Darkness Visible

Darkness Visible

MEMOIR OF A WORLD WAR II COMBAT PHOTOGRAPHER

Charles Eugene Sumners

edited by Ann Sumners

McFarland & Company, Inc., Publishers

Jefferson, North Carolina, and London

Frontispiece: T/5 Charles E. Sumners, 166th Signal
Photo Company, Army Signal Corps, U.S. Army.

Library of Congress Cataloguing-in-Publication Data

Sumners, Charles Eugene.
   Darkness visible : memoir of a World War II combat photographer /
Charles Eugene Sumners; edited by Ann Sumners.
      p.   cm.
   Includes bibliographical references and index.

   ISBN 0-7864-1218-6 (softcover binding : 50# alkaline paper) ∞

   1. Sumners, Charles Eugene.   2. World War, 1939–1945 — Personal
narratives, American.   3. United States. Army — Photographers—
Biography.   4. World War, 1939–1945 — Campaigns— Western Front.
I. Sumners, Ann.   II. Title.
D811.S9124 A3 2001
940.54'8173 — dc21

                                                    2002006620

British Library cataloguing data are available

Cover photograph: Infantrymen of 6th Armored Division, 3rd U.S. Army in Oberdorla,
Germany, chosen as one of the "Best 100 Photos of the European Theater" *(U.S. Army
Signal Corps; photograph by C.E. Sumners)*

Manufactured in the United States of America

McFarland & Company, Inc., Publishers
   Box 611, Jefferson, North Carolina 28640
      www.mcfarlandpub.com

To Sherri, Shane, Pheza, Jacob and
Brad; and to Floyce, the pretty
little girl who became my bride

ACKNOWLEDGMENTS

I am very grateful to Kenny Keiser and David Smith for scanning my photograph collection; and to Rusty White, Bob Sumners and Mark Sumners and my family for their assistance and for encouraging me to undertake this project in the first place.

— *Charles E. Sumners*

CONTENTS

PREFACE

The combat photographer — to understand the nature of this rare breed of GI (who carried a camera, not a gun, into the fight), you must first understand the situations these men were put into and the sacrifices they made in the name of truth and in the cause of documenting a world at war.

The average GI, who carried a rifle and had artillery support, typically participated in one or maybe two battle campaigns. He would be committed to whatever action his particular company, battalion or division was engaged in on the long road from Normandy to Berlin. In between these major campaigns, there was usually time to rest and to regroup before advancing on toward the next inevitable fight.

The combat photographer, in contrast, had his camera, a sidearm and a jeep. Most, including Charles Sumners, claimed an unprecedented five battle stars in this same period of time. He and others in his unit were purposely sent wherever there was fighting, to record and document what happened. This latitude of movement gave the combat photographer a chance to see the war in a scope only imagined by most of the men who fought.

War is a tragedy that falls on top of the everyday lives of the people caught up in it. If that is true, it is also true that within every tragedy is a little comedy. From the unique perspective of the combat photographer, there was many a chance to experience both — from the smell of fresh bread in Ireland to the stench from the ovens at Dachau, and from the tragic climb at Point du Hoc to the jubilant liberation of Paris. These are all vivid memories. Some were captured on film, some simply exist in his memory.

It cannot be forgotten that every situation in every picture that you and I see that shows the cruelty and savagery of war had to be experienced —firsthand — and captured on film by the combat photographer. His life at risk, with little backup and seldom a weapon, he was there to make sure that what happened would not be forgotten.

It is easy, for those of us who have never experienced a war, to look at photographs or film and say how tragic World War II was. Looking back is not so easy for those who were there to fight and for those who were there to witness and record. Charles Sumners has said that some of his best pictures were those he did not take. Surely there is much he wishes he had not seen, but such is the lot of the combat photographer.

This book is a collection of one such man. He would tell you he is no hero, though a Bronze Star says otherwise. He would tell you that he really is not that good a photographer, although a picture of his was selected as one of the top one hundred photographs of the European Theater of Operations (ETO). He would also tell you he was lucky, which five battle stars, a wealth of stories and a fine family will attest to nicely. The following are his memories—and pictures that he did and did not take.

— Ann Sumners

PROLOGUE

My grandson asked me, "Pops, where are you going to start your story?" I told him I guess I would start at the beginning, which was August 15, 1923. I was born to Ernest and Evie Sumners, and delivered by a midwife, Aunt Caroline McGinnis. Named Charles Eugene Sumners, I was the middle child of a large Alabama farm family—the fourth of seven children.

I started school in the old Klein community church that was used during the week as a schoolhouse. After half a year there, I transferred to Vincent (Alabama) School and finished high school there in 1942. I tried to get a job, but no one would hire anyone classified 1-A by the draft board and subject to be called into service soon.

I was drafted by the army in January 1943 and sent to Fort McPherson, Georgia. I was there for four or five days and then sent to Camp Crowder, Missouri. That was my first train ride ever, and it was the first of many types of rides that were to take me to "see the world." That world, during the past 79 years, has provided me with a vault of memories. Some are frightening, some sad, some life-changing; many are happy, but a number are too horrendous to be allowed to surface very often.

This book is a collection of my recollections and photographs of those years that, to borrow from Charles Dickens, were "the best of times, the worst of times"—World War II in the European Theater.

I was a jeep driver and a still photographer in the 166th Signal Photo Company, U.S. Army Signal Corps, attached to the Second Army, First Army and later to General Patton's Third Army when it was activated.

The following are my remembrances.

—*Charles E. Sumners*
Vincent, Alabama
April 2002

1

1

CAMP CROWDER

World War II began for me in January 1943 when 11 guys from Alabama and 11 from Georgia boarded a train at Fort McPherson, Georgia. We left mild weather in the South and arrived in Neosho, Missouri, in the middle of the night with snow of eight to ten inches deep. I thought, "My goodness, they have sent me up here to freeze to death."

At Fort McPherson, we had been issued all our clothes, which included our long underwear. We had said there was no way we were going to wear those things, but we were happy to have those long drawers once we saw how cold it was in Missouri.

The train ride from Georgia to the basic training camp in Missouri was my first train ride, but I'm sure some of the other fellows had ridden one before. Harry Johnson was sleeping in the upper birth of the Pullman car, and when he tried to get down he stepped in Homer Forman's face. Homer said that he always wanted his face rearranged anyway. They became friends out of this encounter. They went through the war together and remained friends all through the years after the war, until Harry's death.

We were supposed to have two weeks of basic training, but, after about five days of sloshing through the ice and snow, I couldn't speak above a whisper or even swallow. I was put in the camp hospital and diagnosed with strep throat; I was running a really high fever. The nurses would come by about every four hours and give me a couple of aspirins, but I never saw the first doctor.

After a couple of days, Lieutenant Furman came over and said to me, "You know we only have three weeks of basic training, and, being in the hospital, you are missing most of it. The rest of your group is about finished, and we are not going to give basic training again for just one man." He gave me the soldier's handbook and told me to read it, memorize it and learn everything that was in there. "When you get out of the hospital," he said, "I will give you a written test, and if you can pass it, that will be your basic training. If you fail it, you'll be sent out to some other company."

I read that book from cover to cover, and I knew everything in there and passed my test with ease. So really, I only had about six or seven days of basic training. I guess you could say I was never a soldier — just a country lad in a GI uniform.

We stayed in the 164th Signal Company for a few weeks and finally were able to get used to the weather conditions in Missouri. I was given the Pfc. rating after about 60 days. Then they transferred us out, as scheduled, for the 166th, and I was given a camera and a T5 rating. Until the war was over, I remained a T5, which was the top rank that a still photographer could make. A movie cameraman could get as high as a tech, a staff, or maybe even a master sergeant.

Camp Crowder is located just outside Neosho, Missouri. This little town had a population of about 500 people, but, after the camp was established, thousands and thousands of soldiers went though there. The camp was situated in an area of eight or 9,000 acres, and there were streets, roads and numerous barracks. Local farmers had owned the property, and the government purchased this land for locating the base. There were many fruit trees and acres upon acres of strawberries left, which GIs would pick for the mess halls.

When I was released from the hospital, I was assigned to the motor pool and given two weeks of drivers training. Mr. Barnes, a civilian instructor, gave us our training, and we were given a drivers test when we finished the school.

The motor pool had jeeps, motor carriers, and 2½-ton trucks. I was given a big truck, and the seat would not adjust to my short legs. I had to find a pillow to put behind my back, so they decided to make me the dispatcher of the motor pool. I typed up trip tickets and sent the drivers off to their duties each morning. My typing was the old hunt and peck method, but I would type them up well in advance. That kept me busy, and I stayed ahead of the game in dispatching the vehicles.

At Camp Crowder we had a post commander — Col. Rinaldo L. Coe — who was a very hard man to deal with. A riding crop from his cavalry days was his trademark, and he was mad at the world.

One Monday morning I was in the motor pool quarters typing my trip tickets (with my hunt and peck system), as it was necessary to type them up several days ahead of time. The motor pool sergeant was on leave, and the motor pool officer was over at the officer's club, probably playing pinochle. Everyone else in the motor pool, drivers and mechanics, was asleep at that time. They were sleeping under vehicles, on benches and all over the place.

I suddenly looked up and saw two officers coming through the door. I jumped to attention and saluted Colonel Coe and a captain. The colonel asked me, "Where is your officer?"

Photograph by Charles Sumners, 166th Signal Photo Company, U.S. Army Signal Corps. Barracks at Camp Crowder, Neosho, MO, 1943.

Camp Crowder, Drivers Training School. Second Army Special Troops. There were ten companies in the school, including two companies of African Americans. Sumners on second row, third from left.

I replied, "Sir, I think he is up at the officer's club or maybe at headquarters."

He said, "You get in touch with him and tell him he has ten minutes to get to this motor pool!" The colonel had already walked through the motor pool and found everyone asleep and had not waked anyone. I called the officer's club, the headquarters, and the orderly room to tell Lieutenant Roche and the First Sergeant that Colonel Coe wanted to see them immediately.

They showed up in about ten minutes, and, by this time, the colonel had all the sleeping soldiers awake and we were all lined up at attention. Colonel Coe chewed and chewed and chewed on both of the officers for some time. He then told Lieutenant Roche, "You take your men for a ten mile forced march after work every afternoon for a week — every man but this one." The colonel then pointed to me and told the lieutenant, "That man was the only one working when I came in, and he's excused."

After chow they put on their full field equipment, their guns and all that stuff. I waved "bye bye" and went on down to the motor pool. I got a 2½-ton truck and went on over the hill and waited for them. I was sitting there by the road as they marched by, and said, "Hey guys, do you want a ride?"

Lieutenant Roche, who was a very nice officer, at first said no but finally said, "Oh, all right. Get in!"

I loaded up the truck with these soldiers and drove them out to the river and we sat there throwing rocks and talking to let time go by. Coming back, they got out of the truck about three blocks from the barracks. I suggested to Lieutenant Roche that maybe he

Weapons carrier pulling itself up a hill via a winch during drills at Camp Crowder, MO, 1943. Charles Sumners in vehicle.

should double-time them the rest of the way so it would look like they had been on a march. He did double-time them. Each day for a week we would follow the same procedure as we had done on the first day. No one ever told or ever found out about this. Lieutenant Roche and I were buddies from then on after that little episode.

Camp Crowder was mostly Signal Corps. Not many people were aware that the Signal Corps was actually started during the Civil War — with a telegraph and pigeons. The army continued to use pigeons even in World War II, and they had a couple of groups in Camp Crowder that were training and taking care of them. These guys were teased a bit about their jobs, but they were good at their work.

They would take the birds miles and miles away — sometimes even 200 or 300 miles from their home base — and release them. The men would bet or have a lottery on whose birds would get back home first. Many times the birds got back before the trainers who released them. The pigeons were let out each morning to exercise, and we would watch them fly by. We were right next to one of the pigeon companies, and they were fun to watch.

They had a pigeon there named "Kaiser" that had been captured by the Allies in World War One. He was about 25 years old at this time, I suppose. He had a German identification tag still on his leg, and they would have had to cut his leg off to remove it.

Another part of training at Camp Crowder was pole line construction, conducted by the 29th Construction Company. There was also a group that handled radio information, a naval detachment, and the women's WAC corps. Not too many of these ladies were pretty — too much GI food, meat and potatoes seemed to do away with their trim bodies. But I must say they looked better than the Russian women that I saw overseas at a later time.

We had our own bakery on the post, and they baked about 18 to 20,000 loaves of bread daily. Our bread was picked up fresh every day, and we were able to get some raisin bread sometimes. I would drive the mess sergeant over to get the bread, and he would take along a pound of butter. We would eat a couple of loaves of this raisin bread on the way back while it was still warm. Now THAT was some FINE eating!

Camp Crowder, Neosho, MO. Baseball game.

2

MANEUVERS

After our training in Camp Crowder, we went on maneuvers in September 1943 to Lebanon, Tennessee. We were billeted in tents on the fairgrounds there and would go out and do some camera work each day. Homer Foreman, Harry Johnson and John Courtney, a boy from Florida, were all in the same tent.

One night Harry and Homer decided they would go into Old Hickory, Tennessee, on a pass. Well, they had put their fatigues out so that they could just jump into them the next morning and fall into formation at the last minute. Courtney and I were sitting around, and I asked him if he knew how to sew.

He said, "Sure, and I've got a needle and thread." We sewed up the bottoms of the pants legs on their fatigues and put them back in place so they would not notice any change.

The next morning we went out there to fall in for our morning formation. Our tent was right behind where we always fell in each morning, and I could see the sides of the tent moving and we could hear mess kits falling. They didn't show up for roll call. About 10:00 the first sergeant sent word up to the motor pool that he needed to see me. I thought, "Oh boy, I am going to catch it now 'cause he has found out what happened."

When I walked in, Sergeant Drake looked at me with a big grin on his face and said, "You know I should give you a month's KP. But that's the funniest damn thing I have heard of in weeks. So you get on back up to the motor pool."

When we first got down to Lebanon, we relieved the fellows in the 164th, and one of these was an ole boy named John Gulley. Gulley said to me, "Charlie, I have a pretty little girl that lives only about three blocks up the street from here. I want you to go up there, tell her who you are and visit with her."

So I got my dress outfit on and headed up there to see her. There was an old man in overalls and a straw hat sitting in a swing on the porch. I went up and told him who I was and asked to see Nellie May. She came to the door. Of course, I'm pretty naive, but

At Camp Crowder, Neosho, MO, 1943. Camera class practice in front of the supply room.

I'm not an idiot. I could see right away that she was well along in the family way. So thinking quickly, I told her that Gulley had sent me up there to tell her that he could not make it up there to see her but he would write to her just as soon as he got back to Camp Crowder.

I told her goodbye and hit the road back to camp. Since ole Gulley was one of those that we replaced, I was not able to find him. I told them that I would probably shoot him if I ever *did* run across him again.

Maneuvers give a fellow a taste of the "real thing" in more ways than war tactics, and personal comfort takes on a new meaning. In the field, the shower consisted of a pipe running out with a canvas stretched up around it, and it would take two guys to

Right: Pfc. Homer L. Foreman on KP duty at Camp Crowder, Neosho, MO, 1943.

take a bath. You would hold the canvas while the other fellow got wet and soaped up, and then he would do the same for you. Then you'd go through the same routine to rinse off.

I became terribly constipated, so I had to go on sick call. When you go on sick call, you have to wear your cartridge belt and canteen. I walked by the motor pool on the way, and Sergeant Alley asked me where I was going. I said, "I'm really constipated, and I'm going on sick call."

He said, "Well, that makes good sense. You're constipated and going on sick call when I have enough laxative right here to work you, the marines, the air force and half the navy!"

When I asked him what he meant, he picked up an old spoon out of the mess kit and wiped it on his old coveralls. He then gave me two spoonfuls of 30-weight motor oil and said, "That's all I ever take for constipation."

I started to leave, and he added, "Now, don't go climbing any trees, because you'll never make it to the ground." I knew what he meant, so I didn't get too far from that old straddle trench that was close by.

Now, you know there are several ways for a fellow to use a straddle trench. If someone is there already, you face him; you never turn the other way. That's just one of the "courtesies" of the army!

L–R: Dwight Kunkle, Nial Alley, Walter Emero — members of the motor pool — on maneuvers in Tennessee, 1943. (Alley gave Sumners the motor oil for constipation.)

Furloughs were always a lot of fun as well as saving a GI's sanity. They offered a chance to touch base with "home" and get away from army regs.

The trains arriving and leaving Camp Crowder were always full of soldiers. Many of them were going home to see wives and family, and there were also many women traveling to see their husbands wherever they were stationed. The train would be crowded, but people were kinder and more helpful back then. You could meet many different people, talk and have a good time traveling on these trains.

I knew a soldier from down home that sent his wife money for train fare to get to visit him. She left home going to the base but met someone on the train that she liked a lot better than her husband. It was a long time before he ever knew what had happened to her, because she never did show up to meet him. That was possibly worse than getting a Dear John letter.

While we were on maneuvers in Tennessee, our first sergeant was on furlough and our motor sergeant, Sergeant Alley, was acting first sergeant. Alley was a friend of mine, and I told him that I would like to go home on a three-day pass. He said, "Fine. I'll give you one, and I'll post-date another one. Then you will have two of the three-day passes; when one pass runs out, the other one will take effect."

I got a bus out of Nashville, Tennessee, to Calera, Alabama. My daddy was working in Calera at that time, so someone picked us up and took us home to Vincent. That was a great four or five days at home before I had to go back.

While I was home, I went over to Childersburg, a town just a few miles away, and bumped into "Polka Dot" Brown. He and I had gone to high school together, and we were totally shocked to find out that we were both stationed at Camp Crowder. We were surprised that we had not run into each other because his outfit and mine even used the same PX. He was such a tall fellow (6'7" or so) that he would surely stand out in a crowd, but we had never seen each other.

We went into Dee's Cafe and though we were in uniform, neither one of us had on a tie and so we were "out of uniform." Suddenly two M.P.s and a Childersburg policeman came in and told us to get up. They took us outside, put us up against the building and began to search us and shake us down. About that time, one of them got a call on the radio. He came back over after answering the call and said, "You fellows can go."

I asked him what was going on. He told us that a real tall soldier and a short soldier had stolen a jeep in Opelika, Ala., and had headed in this direction. They had just been caught in Sylacauga, a town about ten miles over.

As you might guess, that gave us a few anxious moments, and they didn't even notice our missing ties.

Harry Johnson and Homer Foreman lived in Georgia, and we all got furloughs and rode the train home and back to Crowder at the same time. On our trip back to camp, there was a pretty young woman sitting across from us with a young baby.

Harry didn't have any children and was not too fond of kids anyway, but he *was* interested in the mother. So, he asked to hold the baby to let her walk around and get some rest. He took the baby and was bouncing it around and making baby talk, and the mother went to the back of the train. She was gone for a while and then came back and sat down.

There was an empty seat there by her where she had had the baby, and a handsome young soldier came and sat down by her and started talking and laughing with her. Well, Harry was still holding the baby and was getting madder by the minute. He looked around at Homer and me and winked. Then he got up, walked over and put the baby down in this guy's lap saying, "If you are going to court the mama, the least you can do is hold the baby."

The young man didn't know what to do, so the mother took the baby. The guy got up and gave Harry one of those "go to hell" looks. Johnson looked back at him and said, "Better luck next time, son."

Billy Green and I had always heard what a fun town Chicago was. So, we got a three-day pass together and headed to Chicago. When we got off the train, the wind coming off the lake was so strong it would almost blow your clothes off. We had on our overcoats and all the heavy clothes we could get on, and we were still cold.

They had ropes tied along the streets because they were iced over, and holding on to these ropes was the only way you could get from one place to the other without falling down. After three hours there, the weather conditions were so awful that we headed for the train terminal. We took the first train we could find heading back to Camp Crowder.

We had snow on the ground and it was cold at camp. But that was nothing to compare with the snow and cold weather of Chicago. That was my only trip to Chicago.

I had been home on leave for 15 days and was getting in as many dates as I could in this short time that I had at home before shipping overseas. I was practically dating night and day. My mother would get me up early the next day, after my late night dates, to visit relatives and show me off in my uniform to my uncles and aunts. As a result, I didn't get much sleep in those 15 days.

I was headed back to my base at Camp Crowder and had to change trains in Springfield, Missouri. I told the porter that I was a sound sleeper and that I had to have some sleep. I asked him to wake me up to get off the train in Joplin, Missouri, which is close to the base. The porter told me not to worry, that he would make sure that I got off the train in Joplin.

Well, when I finally woke up, I was in Muscogee, Oklahoma, and that's a long way from Joplin. I got off the train at the next stop in some small town and asked the station master when could I get a train back to Joplin. He replied that the next train would be at 11:00 tomorrow.

This was a few minutes before midnight, and I was supposed to be in camp by 6:00 that next morning. I told him that the 11:00 train would get me back too late and that I was going to be AWOL. I walked down to a little cafe that was still open and asked a night watchman if there was any way I could get back to Joplin that night.

Pfc. Harry H. Johnson on KP duty at Camp Crowder, Neosho, MO, 1943.

Billy Green. Camp Crowder, Neosho, MO.

He said that there was a bus that should have already come through there, but had not run yet. He told me to get a cup of coffee and a doughnut and that he would go down to the bus stop and flag down the bus when it came through. He did flag down the bus for me, and I got on — headed back to Joplin.

I finally wound up at camp about 10:00 the next day, four hours late. When I got there, my company was out on an overnight bivouac and had not come back yet. The person in charge of quarters was a friend of mine and told me not to worry. He clocked me in at 6:00, and no one ever knew the difference. That was a close one.

Bill Baker was a soldier who got burned really badly when he got drunk and hugged a hot stove (heater) in the barracks. He was going home, so he told the first sergeant that he was trying to collect all the rank stripes from private to first sergeant. He said that he didn't have first sergeant stripes yet and wondered if the sergeant had an old set of stripes lying around. Sergeant Drayhous — who had been an All-American at Cornell — said, "Yes, I have a set on an old shirt that I never wear anymore. Just take the shirt, cut the stripes off and keep them."

Another guy that lived in Baker's home town came in soon after and showed us a newspaper clipping from their home town paper. There was an article and picture showing "First Sergeant" Baker playing pool in the local pool hall with the mayor of the town!

Ole Baker outsmarted everyone. When we arrived at Camp Kilmer, New Jersey, getting ready to go overseas, he went AWOL. They caught him when he got to Pennsylvania and put him in the guardhouse. He was tried and sent to prison at Fort Leavenworth and was there for a while, until they found out that he had run some big piece of machinery in the Pennsylvania mines before he was drafted.

They needed his services in the coal mines, so they pardoned him to go work on the same job he had before. Baker would then write the boys he knew about all the fun he was having with their girlfriends and wives. Of course, everyone knew he was the biggest liar in the world.

3

SHIPPING OVERSEAS

The Troop Train

In February 1944, I was on a troop train heading out of Camp Crowder to Camp Kilmer in New Jersey, a port of embarkation for overseas. Somehow, I had contracted trench mouth, which is something that affects your gums. Well, I was on this troop train and couldn't get off to get medical attention. When we got to Camp Kilmer, the infection had gone down into my larynx, my throat and tonsils, and I was so sick that they put me in the hospital.

I was on pins and needles, because if you don't ship out with your company, then you go into a replacement pool. From that replacement pool, any company that comes through there that is under strength can draw men — whether it's infantry, artillery or whatever — to get the company or battalion up to strength. So, I faced the possibility of going into that pool.

Lieutenant Moore, our unit officer, came over to see me, and I was much better. I had gotten where I could talk and I could swallow. I could eat but was real weak because I had eaten nothing to amount to anything for about a week. So he talked them into letting me take my medicine and go on with my company. The only two times I have ever been in the hospital in 79 years were at Camp Crowder when I had laryngitis and then later at Camp Kilmer when I had trench mouth. It is highly contagious, and I have yet to know why they let me go on. I guess they figured that I had gotten past the stage where it would be dangerous to anybody else.

So, I came out of the hospital and took all of my shots — seven or nine of them — all on the same day. Both of my arms were so sore I could barely move from all of those shots. Anyway, on February 26, 1944, we boarded the *Susan B. Anthony*, the ship that took us overseas. After about 50 yards starting up the ramp, my duffel bag got so heavy I couldn't carry it, so somebody carried it for me. Later on, somebody took my musette bag. When we

Camp Kilmer, New Jersey, 1944. One of the ports of embarkation for shipping overseas. U.S. Army photograph.

finally got to the ship, there was a guy on either side of me helping me get on the boat, but I shipped out with *my* company! I doctored myself on the way over, and nine days later — when we landed in Ireland — my trench mouth was gone.

Seasick

We crossed the North Atlantic in February 1944, and it was cold. The North Atlantic, of course, is always rough, and many people got seasick. I never got seasick, but I got sick of being at sea. I couldn't eat the food. It had that cold storage kind of "been frozen for weeks" taste about it, and I just couldn't eat it. After we had been out about three days, they opened the ship's stores, and we could go up and buy candy and junk food. So, Jack Apperson and I bought a carton of Milky Ways — 24 bars. We sat down there on the floor — playing pinochle, blackjack or something — and we ate the whole 24 bars. I must have had 15 or better.

When we got to Ireland, they were putting people in the hospital because they were so dehydrated from being seasick. Well, I never got seasick, but I sure did get sick of chocolate.

I don't like chocolate to this day.

4

IRELAND

Ireland was a beautiful country, but our trouble at first was trying to understand the people. In fact, Jack Apperson said, "You sure these people speak English?"

I said, "They speak English, but I'm going to have to listen really close, because so many of the words were so different." Eventually we got the hang of it.

The Maxwell House Castle near Groomsport in Northern Ireland was large enough to take care of 150 men. My entire company, the 166th Signal Photo Company, was billeted in this castle from March 11 to April 25, 1944. There was a beautiful stretch of beach just below the castle where we would go down in the afternoon and spread our blankets on the sandy beach, hoping that some Irish lassies would come by and sit with us. They were shy at first, but eventually they warmed up and were quite friendly — some of them were very pretty and very nice.

In a little town down below, they had a roller coaster, so one afternoon Little Joe Kosoloski and I went downtown. We were standing there watching this roller coaster. It had wooden slats but steel rails, and it went out over the ocean. You could hear it rumble on for about two or three hundred yards when they'd send those cars through there.

Two pretty little Irish girls came up, asking if we wanted to ride. We bought tickets for the four of us and we all got on. I put my arm around this pretty little girl and smiled, and that thing started. I turned her loose and grabbed on for dear life. My hat blew off, and I'd have jumped off; but I looked down, and we were probably 100 feet above the ocean!

We survived, though, and finally, when it stopped and we got off, Little Joe was so sick he had to head for the ocean. I could barely stand up, and I told the girls that I had to go check on my friend. I went down there and he was sick — oh he was *so* sick.

Little Joe got killed later on. He was 19 years old — a friendly, likable little guy. But neither one of us ever took another roller coaster ride!

We were getting our food from the English quartermaster when we were in Northern

16

Ireland. We got a lot of vegetables that I'd never eaten before, and I didn't like them. We got a lot of lamb and, they *said*, Australian beef—but it looked more like the hindquarters of an old horse.

The food was so terrible that I would go over to a little town down the coast, Donnaghadee. They had a little shop over there that sold cookies that were made of artificial flavors and artificial sugar. They were edible, but they were not the best cookies you could find. Next door to the place was a bakery, and that bread smelled so good every time I went there that it would make my mouth water.

One day, this lady was standing in the door of the bakery when I stopped and was sniffing. She was very friendly but said, "I'm sorry, we can't sell you any bread. Everything here is rationed, and we have to account for every loaf of bread that we bake."

I said, "Well, I'd just like to stand here and smell—it smells so good baking that it reminds me of my mama's kitchen."

We talked a little while and finally she said, "Come on in." Well, she whipped around there and rolled me up a small loaf of that bread.

Groomsport, Northern Ireland, March 1944. L–R: Charles Sumners, Larry Lagnell, Jack Apperson — in front of Maxwell House Castle where the 166th Photo Signal Co. was stationed just prior to the Normandy Invasion.

From then on, I'd take her things—margarine, butter, marmalade or anything I could steal out of the kitchen — and swap it to her for bread. I'd bring the bread back and put it in my footlocker to hide it. Everyone else was probably as hungry as I was, so I would slip around to eat my bread.

One day I watched the fishing boats come in. This old Irishman came in, pulled his boat up there and started putting his catch of the day out. I thought, "I'll go down there and buy me some fish. I have a good friend who is a cook at the mess hall. When everybody leaves tonight, I'll go over there, and Whitey and I will have a little fish fry."

So I went down and asked the man if he'd sell me some fish. He said, "No, I won't sell you any fish, but I'll give you some."

I said, "No, I'd like to buy them."

He said, "Oh, no. You don't buy fish." And he gave me four nice fish, the same color as bass. He wrapped them in a white piece of paper and tied them with a string, just like you get them at the grocery store. I put them in the jeep and went back to the barracks. After chow that night, I decided I'd wait until everybody cleared out of the mess hall.

Maxwell House Castle, home of 166th in Groomsport, Northern Ireland, on the shore of the Irish Sea. Two hundred years old and very beautiful. March 1944. U.S. Army Signal Corps; photograph C.E. Sumners.

Now we were living in this old castle, and the mess hall was at the end of a long corridor. Double doors opened up onto this hall, and, as you entered it, the company headquarters (the captain's office, company clerk, so on) was on the left. On down from there, next to the PX, was the mailroom. Our mail clerk always put out an opened bag, so you could just drop mail in. Across the hall was the day room, where you could write your letters, walk out of the room and drop them in the mailbag.

Finally, I decided that everybody had cleared out, and I went over there to get Whitey — so we could clean and fry fish. When I walked in, Jennings, one of the cooks, was there. He didn't like me, and I didn't like him. At one time he had been in the motor pool, and he seemed to think that I was responsible for his getting kicked out of the motor pool and put in the kitchen. He said, "The dining room's closed!"

I said, "Well, where's Whitey?"

He said, "Whitey's gone to town, and there's nothing in here you can have. So you might as well leave!"

I said, "O.K. I was just looking for Whitey."

I started out and, just as I got even with the mailroom, Captain Downs and another officer came in the door. Well, I didn't want to get caught with that package of fish, so I dropped it in the mailbag, gave a salute and went on out. I thought they'd go in there for a minute or two, then I'd slip back in there and get my fish. I waited and waited and waited. They didn't come out, so I thought, "I'll get up early in the morning and come over and get them."

Waiting for mail: T/5 Charles Sumners, 166th Signal Photo Co., U.S. Army Signal Corps. Sumners had this picture made and sent a copy to everyone he knew to let them know he needed mail.

About 2:30 A.M., Sam Rondone, Charge of Quarters, came over and woke me up. He said, "You and Arthur Statt [a still photographer] have to drive down to Engineer Company. They're going to put on a demonstration, and he has to photograph it. You'll eat breakfast down there, and you're leaving now."

I thought, "Oh, goodness sakes. Maybe I've got time to run over and get that fish out of the mailbag." But when I came outside, Statt was already sitting in the old weapons carrier waiting for me. So we headed about ten or 15 miles down there and had breakfast with this engineering outfit. They put on their demonstration, and he made pictures until about 9:00 or 10:00 o'clock. We loaded up, headed back and got back around 10:30–11:00.

Harry Johnson was the headquarters driver, and he was standing by his jeep when we drove up. I looked out there and saw the mailbag hanging on the clothesline. Harry said, "Slick, you missed it."

I said, "What's going on, Harry? Why's the mailbag hanging on the line?"

He said, "Elmo Scott [the mail clerk] said if he could find out which one of those Pennsylvania Pollock bastards tried to mail that fish home, the company might have its first casualty." He added, "It's a good thing you weren't here, Slick, or they may have blamed that on you."

I said, "You're right, Harry. I'm glad I wasn't here."

"Goon Platoon" on KP duty in Northern Ireland. March, 1944. L–R: Sgt. Jennings, the cook, overseeing Pvt. Lickenfelt and Pvt. Pearson.

We had this big ole boy in Ireland who decided he didn't want any more of the army, he didn't want to be in the invasion, and he didn't want to go to war. He walked around with his chin about eight inches off the ground and with "terrible back pains." He'd go on sick call *every* morning, and this went on for about a month. They'd checked him and x-rayed him and everything. Finally the docs called the company commander and said, "There's nothing wrong with this fellow Creath that you keep sending over here — he's goldbricking. Don't send him down here anymore, because there's nothing we can do for him. He's just as sound as he can be."

Well, the commander called Creath in and told him, "You know that we're over here for the invasion of France, and you know it's not too far into the future. If your back does not get straight within the next two or three days, I'm going to transfer you out to an infantry company and tell them to make sure that you are the first American soldier to hit the beach in France."

Ole Creath straightened up, and he hasn't had a pain since. Seems the company commander had miraculously cured Creath of his back problem.

We had a young man from Virginia. He wrote his girlfriend every night. He was *so* in love. He had her picture — a pretty little blond-headed girl — and he carried it everywhere he went. She was all he ever talked about, and he never looked at another girl. He never went to the PX. He never went out anywhere. He would just stay there and write his girlfriend.

We'd been in Ireland about three weeks when he got a "Dear John" letter. She had married one of his friends (they'd all gone to high school together). She said she was sorry, but had decided she didn't want to wait 'til he got back. So, he got dressed and went down to a little pub about a mile or two from camp.

I was on guard duty that night, and I heard this terrible noise coming from down the road. This old boy had stolen a bicycle. He was drunk, and he'd fall over about every fifteen feet. Then he'd get back up and get back on that bicycle. I got him off the bicycle, finally got him inside, and stood the bicycle up out there by the guard shack.

Art Creath.

The next morning, the Irish police came by and saw the bicycle, and they asked how it got there. I said, "I don't know. It just happened to show up." I don't know if they believed me or not, but they took the bicycle back.

He became a regular soldier after that. He would go around chasing women and drinking. It didn't take him too long to get over the "Dear John" letter.

5

ENGLAND

Sometimes people ask, "Why does God allow war?" I don't know the answer to this, but war is a terrible thing, sometimes a necessary thing, that dramatically affects everyone involved. Sometimes war has meaning, and sometimes it has none. However, there is one constant: Those who suffer the most have nothing to gain from its outcome and had nothing to do with starting it.

The British people have my admiration for being the most courageous of all the people involved in World War II. Hitler and the German command would not believe that they could fail to whip England with their superior German Air Force. They had not factored in the determination of the RAF pilots or the courage of the British people.

The Nazis sent wave after wave after wave of bombers and escort fighter planes to bomb the waterfront docks and to try to knock out the radar stations along the coast. Then they started bombing the towns, especially London, killing thousands of civilians. The British people endured 57 consecutive nights of those air raids—night after night on many of the same targets. In the morning, they would clear the rubble, treat the wounded and remove the dead for burial. They would then get ready for the next night's raids.

Our company was transferred to Moberly Station, England (near Manchester), in April 1944 to await orders to join other forces for the invasion of France. We later moved to the southern port area of England near Portsmouth and shipped out for the beaches of Normandy.

I talked to many English people who had lived through those terrible raids and had seen the streets the next morning. One girl that I knew worked in a defense plant ten hours a day. Then she worked a four-hour shift with the antiaircraft group before going to sleep in an air raid shelter. She would get up each morning, have a cup of tea, eat a biscuit and start another day—the same routine all over again.

The Germans had many more planes than the British, but the radar system that

House in Moberly Station, England. Sumners' unit was billeted in this house awaiting transportation to Normandy. This photograph was taken on a visit back to Europe in 1977.

England had was very effective in evening the odds. Radar helped the British pinpoint where the German planes were coming from, so the RAF fighter planes would be up in the air to meet them. The RAF pilots would fly mission after mission until they were exhausted, and they were able to shoot down many of the German planes before they reached London. The German High Command lost much of its air force superiority trying to defeat England with their air power.

Of course, we know that the Jewish people suffered the most in Germany, Poland and throughout Europe. From 1933 until 1945, the Germans killed, or put into labor camps, millions of Jews. In Poland alone, three million Jews were killed. One out of every 19 Polish people lost their lives during this time. Many of the Jews that lived in Germany prior to World War II tried to flee the country. Some of them were able to make it out, but most did not.

One person who did get out was Arthur Herz who, after the war, formed a photography school in Rochester, New York. He escaped from Germany through Switzerland to Italy and finally got to the United States. He tried to enlist in the navy, the air force and the marines, but was turned down each time. He finally joined the army as a photographer and was assigned to our company, the 166th.

He was wounded in a German town while trying to talk the people into surrendering to the Americans to avoid more bloodshed. He could speak fluent German and was out in the street talking when a sniper shot him in the back. (This story is detailed elsewhere in this book.) Art is alive today and lives in Rochester.

The Dirty Dozen

The book *The Dirty Dozen* was written by E.M. Nathanson. This was a very well-written book that was later made into a movie starring Lee Marvin, Jim Brown and several other well-known actors. This was an excellent movie and can still be seen on reruns on television.

The original idea for the story came from Russ Meyer while he and Nathanson were sitting in a bar in Los Angeles one night. Russ told Nathanson about the time that Russ and I had gone down to a stockade in England and spent a couple of days photographing there. The story in the book was either Meyer's or Nathanson's version of the affair, but Meyer received ten thousand dollars for telling Nathanson the story of this stockade that led Nathanson to write his book.

There were many prisoners at this stockade at the time. Some were locked up in cells while others were on the grounds tossing a softball or just sitting around smoking and talking. It was a stockade with barbed wire across the top of the fence, and guards carried live ammunition.

We ate in the same mess hall with the prisoners, but well away from them at a table with the noncoms and the guards over in a corner. The thing that I remember most was that the prisoners were not allowed to talk in the mess hall, except to ask for salt to be passed if needed. So you see, it was almost total silence in the mess hall.

My memory was that there were some mean-looking men in that stockade, and I did not want to get too close to any of them. Those locked in isolation cells were only let out to exercise or eat chow. They ate at a separate table, and wore leg shackles at all times to prevent escape. I think the basis for the "selected dozen" came from Meyer's description of these shackled men.

We slept in a hut that was located just outside the stockade where a corporal, a sergeant and some privates stayed. There was also a shack type of building where the commanding officer and the officers stayed. A colonel, a captain and a couple of lieutenants stayed there.

The prison was located in a rather remote area, so not a lot was going on around there. When Meyer finished filming, we were told that the colonel wanted the film. They not only took the film that was exposed, but also took the unexposed film that was in my musette bag as well. So, there was no record of this visit.

Nathanson wanted to tell the story and to shoot the movie as factual, but the army denied any knowledge of the stockade. They said it never happened and that there was no such place.

He called me from California on two or three occasions in 1962 asking me for details of this visit. While I was out in California visiting Meyer a few years ago, we had dinner with Nathanson, and he was still asking us questions about this subject. This event happened in 1944, so my memory was not too detailed, but I do know that we spent one night and two days at this stockade that the army denies existed, and we had shot film that was confiscated before we left.

The Officers' Liquor Ration

After we left Moberly Station near Manchester, we moved down to the south of England and were there for a few weeks. The officers were issued liquor rations, and they were to come from back in Manchester where we had been. Lieutenant Moore, my unit officer, said "I'll take Charlie, and we will go back and get the liquor rations."

We drove back up to the depot in Manchester, got the liquor rations and, of course, he had to sample some of it immediately. We decided to stay the night and headed out early the next morning, getting back down to the base camp around one o'clock that afternoon.

The company was gone by that time, and there was no military around. We didn't know where they had gone or how to get in touch with them. We knew that wherever they were, finding them would be very difficult because the general destination was embarkation points for the invasion of Europe. There would be millions of soldiers and hundreds of units. Lieutenant Moore almost had a heart attack and was wringing his hands, wondering what we were going to do.

About that time, I noticed a young girl riding toward us on a bicycle, and she waved at me. I started out to meet her, and Lieutenant Moore yelled at me, "Sumners, where in the hell are you going? We don't know where the company is, and you are out there chasing a girl!"

I went on out there, and she gave me a piece of notebook paper. On the paper was our exact route, showing where we were going, with locations of the towns we would be going through and everything mapped in detail. We don't know who had drawn this map and given it to this young girl to give to us, but it's very surprising since everything about army movements during war is always very secret.

I took the note with the map drawing over to Lieutenant Moore and told him that I now knew where we were going. We headed out, following the map and driving as fast as roads would permit us, and we finally caught up with them after about 30 miles.

Several weeks before that, they had given us a kit to waterproof our jeeps in case we landed in high water going in during the invasion. There was a pipe sticking up from the carburetor that would provide air for the engine in case we needed it. They also provided a heavy, gunky tar type of substance that was to be put over the spark plugs to waterproof them for beach landings.

I had not prepared my jeep at this time,

Charles Sumners, April 1944. En route from Manchester, England, to the invasion embarkation area of Southern England, Sumners waterproofs his jeep.

T/5 Charles Sumners, 166th Signal Photo Company, with his jeep, Moberly Station, England, April 1944. On the back of this photograph, Sumners wrote, "My jeep — now named 'Couché Avec,' French for 'Slept With.' The girls giggle when they see it. I just laugh out loud."

even though I had had the kit for a few days. Every time we stopped for a break, I would get out and work on the jeep, putting this old heavy tar looking gunk on the spark plugs and other such items under the hood of the jeep.

When we finally got to where we were going, I had my jeep pretty well waterproofed. However, when we got to France, I found out that I did not need all that junk on my jeep. That boat ran up to the beach, let the front end down, and we drove onto the sand with as much ease as if there was not a drop of water around.

6

WAR IS EVIL

War is an evil, but sometimes a necessary evil. We paid a terrible price in World War Two: 16,353,659 men and women were in the armed forces and of that group 282,131 were killed in combat, 115,185 died of noncombat wounds, and 670,846 were wounded in action.* There were countless numbers that were prisoners of war and many that could never be accounted for. The United States paid a big price in losses, but it was small when you consider what some other countries' losses were.

Poland was one such country. One out of every 19 Polish people was killed during the war, and 90 percent of the 3.3 million Polish Jews were murdered. Poland was defeated in a short period of time, and this was just the beginning of Hitler's assault on Europe.

The German war machine in Europe consisted of a well-trained mechanized army and the Luftwaffe. All Poland had to counter this with was an old horse-drawn military machine. Their finest fighting troops were their cavalry, and you can't fight tanks with cavalry. But they fought as long as they could and suffered a bitter, bitter defeat. Poland had depended on help from France and England, but help did not get there in time to save them from being taken over by the Germans.

The United States entered the war, not because we wanted to, but because we had to. Hitler had to be stopped. After the Japanese bombed Pearl Harbor, Hitler declared war on the United States. Our leaders decided that we needed to defeat Hitler first, and then we would defeat Japan. Thus a lot of the American troops and resources were concentrated on defeating Hitler and the Germans. It was decided that the way to proceed was through Sicily, Italy, North Africa, and then later with the invasion of France.

The German army was well trained, well equipped and a very good fighting force. I think that the big difference between the German soldier and the American soldier was

*"The Price." American Legion Magazine, September 1991, p. 128.

27

that the German soldier was trained to do exactly as he was ordered, while the Americans were not as well trained, but they would do things on their own without specific orders. Americans would improvise and make decisions in the field to overcome obstacles before them. The German soldiers would wait for orders before they did anything. If something happened to their sergeant or officer in charge, they would be at a standstill and could not function.

Germany had what it called the Blitzkrieg (lightning war), a strategy which involved the air force razing a target to the ground. They subjected Poland to a merciless Blitzkrieg. Their planes had something on the wings that made a terrible noise when they came in. It was a frightening thing to hear these German bombers come in like that, and I'm sure they worked on the nerves of everyone. They used this same strategy in Belgium, Holland and France.

Hitler had signed a pact with the Soviet Union. He wanted Germany allied with Russia before they entered Poland, to make sure the Russians would not intervene. The Russians were responsible for many atrocities, as were the Germans. The Russians captured

German troops parade through Warsaw, Poland. September 1939. National Archives at College Park, MD; photograph by J. Hugo.

thousands of Polish troops while they were allied with Germany and did many terrible things to these troops and to Polish civilians. Hitler later invaded Russia, so the Russian government was not charged with all of their war crimes like the Germans were.

The Treaty of Versailles was signed at the end of World War I, and the conditions laid on Germany were pretty tough. The treaty humiliated the proud German people, and they felt it was unjust and too harsh a penalty to pay. Then, to make matters worse, the Great Depression hit ten years after the treaty went into effect. During this atmosphere of defeat and protest, Hitler was able to come into power in 1933, and he soon became an absolute dictator.

Hitler had a furious hatred for Jews, and he felt the German people were superior to all other humans. He convinced the German people that they were the super race, and he even started programs early to produce a super race. He set up camps where he would have his best-trained, most physically healthy officers be available to impregnate their very best-looking, healthy blonde German girls. These women were sent to these camps to breed his super race of people.

The children born of these unions were Hitler's prized kids. They were sent to special schools to learn military tactics and how to survive in war. They were 12 to 14 years of age when World War II began and they were very dedicated to Hitler and Germany's cause. Toward the end of the war they fought alongside elderly German men. Although some of them were as young as ten, they were pretty good soldiers because they had been trained since youth and were able to do what most of the other soldiers did.

At the Treaty of Versailles, the Germans had been blamed for starting World War I. A map was drawn up giving much of the German territories to France and Belgium, and the Rhineland was occupied by troops of the winning nations. A great portion of original German land occupied by German-speaking people was given away at this treaty. Hitler was determined to get all this land back, plus a lot more for the insults on the German people in this treaty.

Under the Treaty of Versailles, the German army was supposed to be kept small at about 100,000 soldiers, but Hitler slowly and secretly built it up despite this treaty limitation. He built up his navy as well. He declared that Germany needed more living space and had to expand, and he did this by taking other territories—one at a time. In 1936, Germany occupied the Rhineland and then annexed Austria in 1938. They then took Czechoslovakia.

It was logical, at least to Hitler, that the Republic of Poland was next in line for a takeover. This would return Danzig,

T/5 Charles Sumners, 166th Signal Photo Company, Signal Corps, U.S. Army, looks at a French grave with a picture of St. Bernadette. Photograph by Cpl. Lou Crabtree, 1944.

A Russian graveyard from World War I, in France, 1944. T/5 Charles Sumners reads the inscriptions. U.S. Army Signal Corps. Stamped: "Passed for Publication. Field Press Censor. 1 OCT 1944."

Poland, to Germany and give back Germany's freedom to move across the Polish border to East Prussia.

Both England and France were supposed to be watching what was going on in Europe. When Germany took Czechoslovakia in 1939, Great Britain and France were beginning to wonder if Hitler would turn toward the West as his prime target. They were alarmed, but they didn't do anything.

As Hitler moved east toward Russia, the Soviets—who were allied with Britain and

France — became alarmed by this aggression. In Moscow, on the night of August 23, 1939, they signed the Nazi-Soviet Pact with Germany (in which the parties agreed not to go to war with each other). This, the Soviets thought, was insurance against a Nazi attack.

After Hitler signed the nonaggression pact, he knew then that he could take over Poland without interference from Russia. Then Germany and Russia would divide the country of Poland between them. This was all the assurance Hitler needed. He was ready to take over Poland, and he did.

The Polish people were at the mercy of the Russians on one side of their country and the Germans on the other side. The Polish army did not last long. Their old outdated, World War I equipment could not stand up to the new modern German weapons, and the German air force also had control of the sky. Of course, the German army was efficient in everything it did. With their tanks, bombers, and the Blitzkrieg, it didn't take them long to wade through Poland.

It is hard to explain to families that lost a son, husband or father just exactly what the cost of the war was. For instance, we had a man in my company whose father was dead. All his mother had left were her two sons. Randy Richmond was in our unit and received word that his brother had been killed in the fighting in the Pacific Theater. Three or four weeks later, Randy was killed in France. What price could be quoted to that lady?

Randy was among the first unit casualties of the 166th Photo Company. Statistics show that one of every four combat photo cameramen did not survive World War II. I have been told by several sources that we were probably the most decorated company in the European Theater. I don't know that to be a fact, but we had many killed and many wounded.

So, yes — war is a terrible thing.

7

PHOTOGRAPHERS

After we first left Utah Beach, our unit was working with First Army, 28th Infantry. Third Army had not yet been activated. They were really just a paper army, and it wasn't until sometime in July that they finally gave General Patton the division he needed to form the Third Army. We then began documenting their combat.

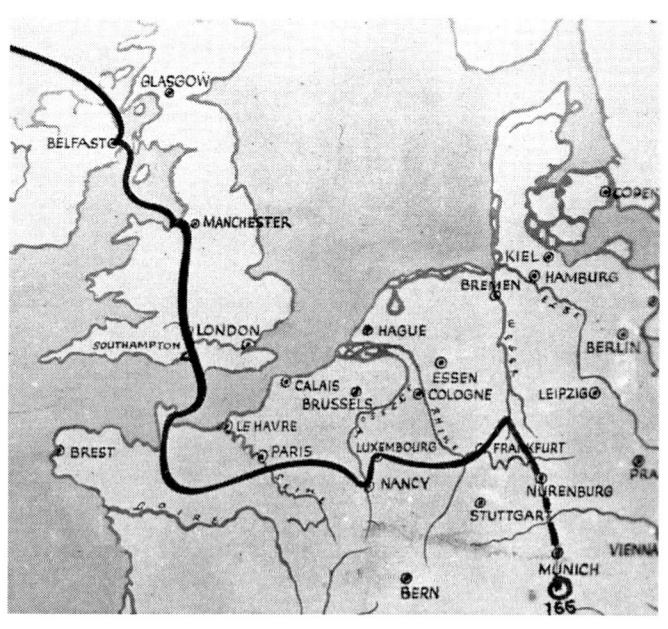

Published in the weekly newspaper by 166th Signal Photo Company. Roughly the route covered in the ETO by the 166th.

The 166th had 20 to 25 officers. Each photo unit had an officer in charge, and that unit would be attached to various divisions. Our unit was never attached to any one division; rather, we were usually sent on special assignments to wherever the action was. Because of this, we were most likely in more combat situations than any other unit.

The other units were assigned only to a certain division and were in a position to take combat pictures only when that division was in a combat situation. Sometimes these divisions were holding a line on the front and other times they

Camera class taught by Lou Crabtree and Charles Sumners. Cheligny, France, 1945. L–R: Joe Scrippens, Miles Landum, Lou Crabtree, Walter Romero, Robey Richey. The camera is a 4×5 Speed Graphic. Photograph by C.E. Sumners, 1945.

might be in reserve in the rear to regroup and replace casualties before going back to the front lines. So, there were times when the other photo units did not have a situation where they could take combat pictures.

I was fortunate that I served with some good people. There were 11 people in my original unit: Lieutenant Gene Moore, Sergeant Gene Abrams, Sergeant Ralph Butterfield, Sergeant Harry Downard, Sergeant Russ Meyer, Sergeant Robert Brill, Corporal Charles Sullivan, Corporal Charlie Sumners, Corporal Joe Lapine, Corporal Lou Crabtree, and Private Gordon Patmon.

Lapine was a good still photographer and a fine young man, and he really wanted to do the job. But his nerves just would not let him and they sent him back to the company. We tried five or six other "still" men, but I was the only one of the "stills" who started and stayed with my outfit until the end

Walter Romero.

The original 11 members of Sumners' unit of 166th Signal Co. Top: Charles Sumners, Gordon Patmon; Middle: Bob Brill, Harry Downard, Gene Moore, Russ Myers, Ralph Butterfield, Gene Abrams. Bottom: Joe Lapine, Lou Crabtree, Charles Sullivan.

of the war. We had Sullivan, Crabtree, Lapine, Mike Marder, Willy Breedlove and Gordon Patmon. Walter Romero joined us about one month before the war ended.

We were supposed to be a newsreel unit, with a big soundtrack and camera. This did not work out, however, as the noise of the artillery would just blow the sound system all to pieces. Finally they abandoned the sound system and broke the 11 men crews into smaller units. Later on, as more troops came and the action spread over Europe, they split us up even more into small four-man and three-man units. After crossing the Moselle River, my unit consisted of Lieutenant Moore, Sergeant Meyer and me. I was the driver as well as the still photographer.

Because we were a floating type of unit sent to wherever there was something newsworthy enough going on, we would jump from one division to another or from one area to another. When action at one front cooled down, we would move to another, and our Eisenhower passes allowed us access to wherever we needed to go.

Lieutenant Moore was my unit commanding officer, and after a while he more or

Willie Grogan and Gene Abrams, 166th Signal Photo Co.

less gave Russ Meyer and me free rein to set our schedule to go where we wanted to go and do what we wanted to do to get action combat pictures. Many times, Lieutenant Moore did not even know where we were. When we got back from shooting our pictures, we would check back in with him to let him know what we had been doing.

Taking the film back to headquarters at night was about as dangerous as going up to the front, because you never knew when some trigger-happy road guard 20 miles behind the lines would shoot you. You made sure to know the password, and you had to be really careful since you were driving blacked out with no lights on. It could be very scary to take our film back on these strange roads with all these obstacles to contend with.

We would take the film back to the message center, and they would then send it to Army Pictorial Services. In the early part of the war right after the invasion, pictorial services headquarters was located in London. Later on, after Paris was liberated, the headquarters was there. That really helped speed up the process. We could make a combat picture and 36 hours later, it would be in a newspaper, magazine or shown in the theaters in the states.

When our film was sent to Army Pictorial Services, there would be at least five prints made—one for the photographer, one for the news pool, one for Signal Photo Company, one for Army Photo Section and one for the Army Pictorial Services files. The print sent back from Army Pictorial Services would have the captions, the credits and all the information printed on the back of the photograph.

I didn't understand the technology of how they could radio a combat picture back to the states. This was before television and was probably one of the first attempts at sending pictures over sound waves. I would make a combat picture, and Pictorial Services would radio it back to the states. Two days later it might be in a newsreel, a magazine or a newspaper. The copy that I received would be stamped on the reverse: "RADIO."

Only occasionally, we might find out if and where the photography was used. One of my photos was published in the *New York Herald Tribune*, and someone later sent me a copy of the paper.

Many times we would get a print back that only had the words "Confidential—Not

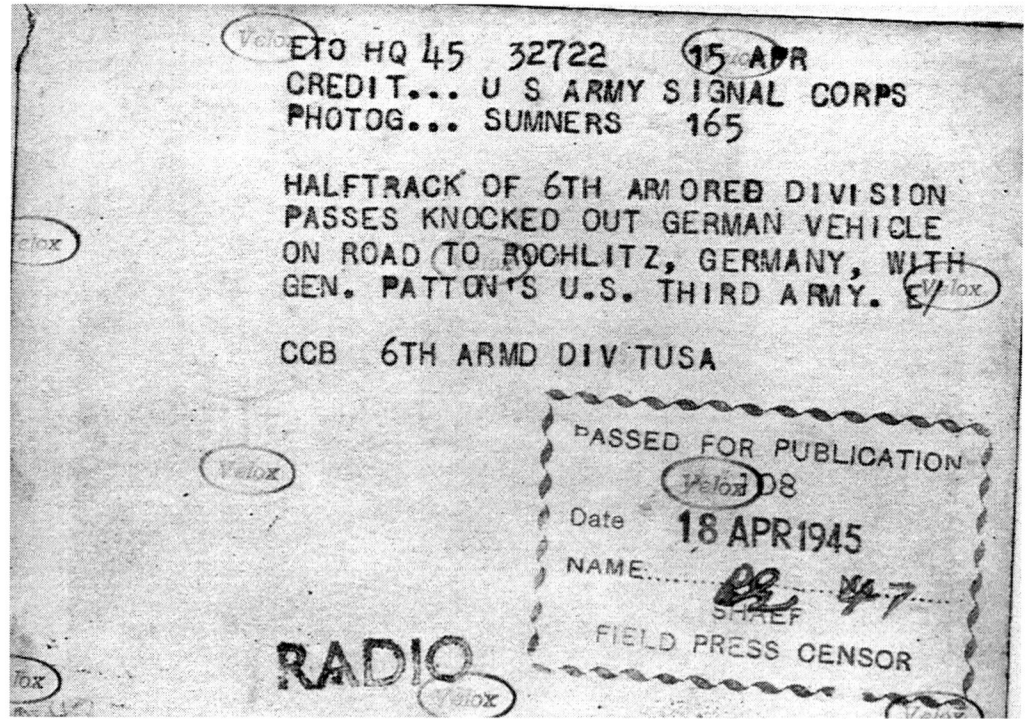

Reverse of photograph showing captions and censor marks. "RADIO. Passed for Publication."

Photograph printed in *New York Tribune Herald*. April 1945. Street in Mülhausen, Germany. U.S. Army Signal Corps; photograph by C.E. Sumners.

to Be Published — Field Press Censor" stamped on the back. At other times, the information would be there, but certain words would be marked through with blue marker to indicate that the marked words could not be used in the captioned information. Those would be stamped: "Passed for Publication as Censored. Field Press Censor."

You could look at it and not really see why, but I guess that there may have been something in the particular picture or descrip-

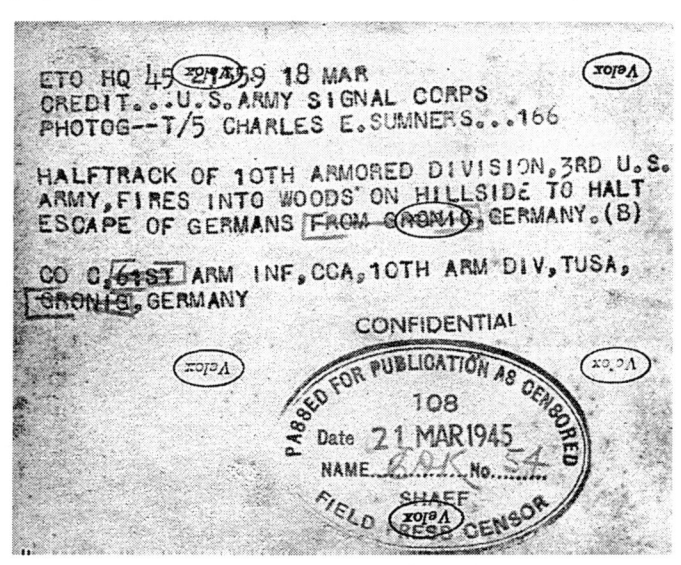

Reverse of a typical photograph showing captions and censor marks. "Passed for Publication as Censored."

ETO HQ 45   20108   15 MAR
CREDIT - U.S. ARMY SIGNAL CORPS
PHOTOG - CPL C.H. SUMNERS   166

RUSSIAN FAMILY RECENTLY LIBERATED BY
U.S. TROOPS WHEN THEY MOVED INTO THE
SECTOR NEAR TRIER, GERMANY, GATHER
ROUND A FIRE COOKING THEIR EVENING
MEAL IN A DISPLACEMENT CAMP OPERATED
BY MILITARY GOVERNMENT TEAM. FROM HERE
THE PEOPLE ARE RETURNED TO THEIR HOME
LANDS.   (X)

TRIER, GERMANY

PASSED FOR PUBLICATION
108
Date
NAME
SHAEF
FIELD PRESS CENSOR

Reverse of photograph showing captions and censor marks. "Passed for Publication" as is.

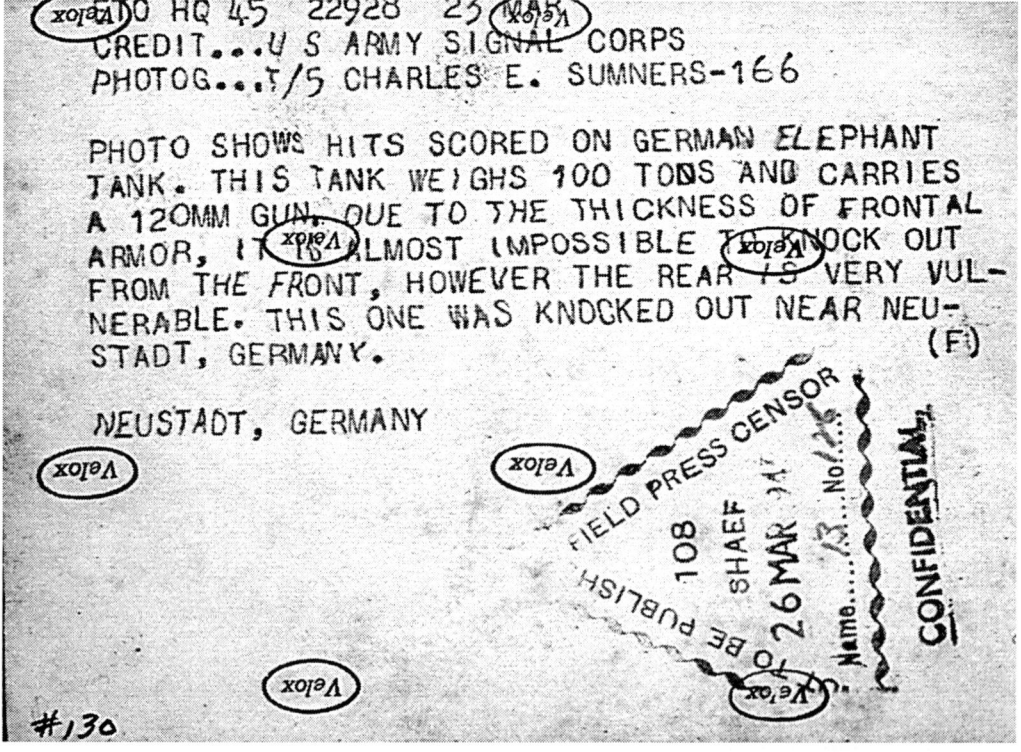

ETO HQ 45   22928   25 MAR
CREDIT...U S ARMY SIGNAL CORPS
PHOTOG...T/5 CHARLES E. SUMNERS-166

PHOTO SHOWS HITS SCORED ON GERMAN ELEPHANT
TANK. THIS TANK WEIGHS 100 TONS AND CARRIES
A 120MM GUN. DUE TO THE THICKNESS OF FRONTAL
ARMOR, IT IS ALMOST IMPOSSIBLE TO KNOCK OUT
FROM THE FRONT, HOWEVER THE REAR IS VERY VUL-
NERABLE. THIS ONE WAS KNOCKED OUT NEAR NEU-
STADT, GERMANY.   (F)

NEUSTADT, GERMANY

FIELD PRESS CENSOR
108   SHAEF   26 MAR
TO BE PUBLISH
Name   No.
CONFIDENTIAL

#130

Reverse of photograph showing captions and censor marks. "Confidential. Not to Be Published."

tion that, in the wrong hands, could give the enemy information they could use against us. I did get a lot of prints back from Army Pictorial Services that were stamped "Censored" on the back.

Our photographs were also evaluated to give us feedback. The print sent back would show crop marks (white lines and arrows) to indicate that the evaluator thought the photographer should have been at a certain spot when

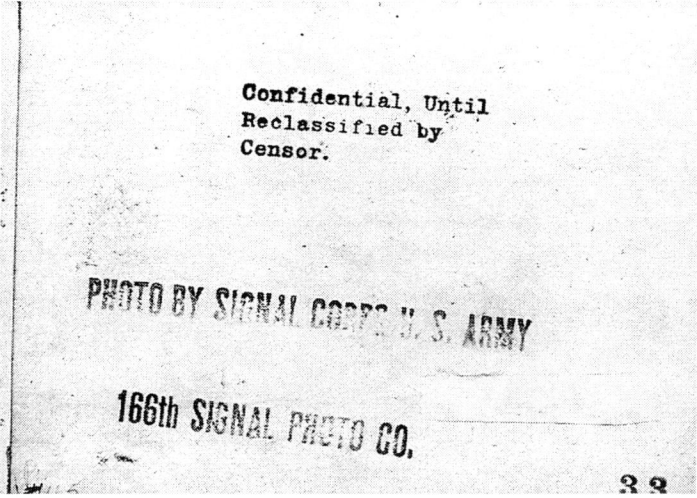

Reverse of photograph showing captions and censor marks. "Confidential, Until Reclassified by Censor."

taking it. Moving up closer for the shot, in most cases, would have made it better, but many times it would also have exposed the photographer to open fire.

Typical scene of combat, Wedern, Germany. Markings indicate where the evaluator thinks Sumners should have been to get a better photograph. That would have meant being exposed in the open. These GIs are behind a stone wall for protection from snipers. U.S. Army Signal Corps; photographer C.E. Sumners.

Two infantrymen of the 3rd U.S. Army catch a few winks in their jeep on the outskirts of the burning town of Waldkeppel, Germany, taken by elements of the 6th Armored Division during the 3rd Army drive. U.S. Army Signal Corps; photograph by C.E. Sumners. Stamped: "Confidential. Passed for Publication as Censored. Field Press Censor. 5 APR 1945."

Meyer and I were on one of our assignments when I saw a jeep on the road. It was directly in the road, with two GIs sitting in it sound asleep. I stopped my jeep, got my camera out of the case, and made a picture of this scene of tired soldiers.

We drove on to our location and sent the film with this picture to Army Pictorial Service. They sent me an ugly critique back telling me that I was wasting film on things like this and that this was not the type of picture that we were sent out to take.

Weeks later, I saw this exact picture in the *Stars and Stripes* or some other publication. They had used my picture, which I had thought was a good picture, for a human interest story. You just never knew, when you took a picture, what would be acceptable, or if and where it might be used.

8

ST. LÔ

St. Lô was the first rough combat that we had gotten into. Before that we had only taken photographs after the action. Usually it had just been little French towns, and we were fairly well behind the infantry.

St. Lô was an important town for both the Allied troops and the Germans. The 28th Infantry had taken the town, and the Germans counterattacked and kicked us out. We went back in again; then they took the town again.

Russ Meyer and I were back doing our captions. At the end of each day, we would have to write our captions and get our film in a press bag to be sent back to the message center. They would then send it to the pictorial center that would process the film and classify it. If it were newsworthy, it would be radioed back to the states.

While we were doing this, word came of our first casualties — we had lost one entire photography unit. Lieutenant Shadden and Sergeant Richmond were killed. Walker and Sloan were both wounded. It finally occurred to us that a photographer could be killed just as easily as a tanker or someone in the infantry. In fact, one out of every four combat photographers did not survive the war. This had a sobering effect on us.

Meyer called me aside and asked me, "What are we going to do? We are supposed to go down the hill with the infantry in the morning."

I said, "I've already decided. If we do *not* go down the hill to St. Lô in the morning with the infantry, we won't be worth a damn for the rest of this war." We shook hands on it, and we've been friends ever since.

Our troops took St. Lô, and, as we went down the hill the next morning, we could see where all the road's blacktop had been destroyed by artillery and mortar shells. As we went down a dirty, muddy road approaching the town, to the left was a huge apartment building approximately six stories high. A sniper shooting out of that building wounded a couple of infantrymen. After they took the building, they discovered the sniper's body on the third or fourth floor — the sniper was a woman.

They tied a bed sheet to one of her legs and tied it to a bed or something inside. Then they hung her out of the window — upside-down — with her gown and hair hanging down and her body riddled with bullet holes. This was for a warning to other snipers, I suppose, but it also made a lasting impression on me to see this young woman hanging out of the window of that apartment building.

This was a decisive victory for the Allied forces. This infantry division that took the town had been in combat since the landings at Normandy. We observed them after this battle as they were being relieved by fresh troops, and they looked like walking zombies. These hardened, veteran troops had the appearance of troops that had been in battle too long. They came marching out of there not as conquering heroes but like a group of soldiers that had lost everything. They had been through so much combat that they were just completely washed out — totally spent. They would look at you and not really see you.

This was the life of the infantryman — completely worn out from extensive battle

Wrecked German equipment burns along road near Frankenstein, Germany, as infantrymen and armor of the 10th Armored Division lead U.S. Army advance toward the front. U.S. Army Signal Corps; photograph by C.E. Sumners. Stamped: "Passed for Publication. 24 MAR 1945."

time; but after some rest, they would return to combat. They had to go through rain, sleet, snow, mud and extremely cold weather. They also had to endure artillery attacks, bombing raids and intense fighting for weeks on end. It was not an easy life, and they could easily be killed at any time. They were the ones who bore the brunt of the war.

Of course, we lost people in the air force and on ships at sea, but usually they died with a full stomach and hadn't endured the suffering that the old "foot slogger" had to endure. Indeed, the infantryman had my utmost respect, because he had gone through so much; he never backed up; he just kept going, knowing that tomorrow he might "buy the farm."

And that's the way it went.

Infantrymen of the 80th Division, 3rd U.S. Army, march through forest ravine as they return from mission near Frankenstein, Germany. They have just cleared nearby mountainside of enemy troops. The soldiers were working with the 10th Armored Division. U.S. Army Signal Corps; photograph by C.E. Sumners. Stamped: "Passed for Publication. Field Press Censor. 24 MAR 1945."

Gen. Patton's 3rd Army. Armored infantry column advancing. Truck is pulling ammo trailer. Tripod on soldier's back is for a B.A.R. automatic weapon (too heavy to carry both). Dead horse, left foreground. Smoke hovers over the area. U.S. Army Signal Corps; photograph by C.E. Sumners. Stamped: "Confidential, Until Reclassified by Censor."

9

NEHOU

After the battle at St. Lô, we were called back to the company near the little French town of Nehou. We were looking for the Third Army to be activated just any day, and then we would be assigned to one of its divisions. So far, we had never been assigned to any specific division or unit, but worked with all of the armor and infantry units of the First Army. For a while we even worked with the cavalry, which was kind of a scary outfit. We were never really assigned, but were just given job after job after job wherever there was a push going on or wherever there was a hot spot in the fighting that was newsworthy or worth photographing.

We billeted just outside of town in an apple orchard with the trucks all backed into the edge of the woods, and the meadow was wide open. While we were waiting word of an assignment, we were given company details to do, one of which was the water detail.

Soldiers were not allowed to drink the water in France because of all the impurities in it at that time. Our detail would go to the water point and get the supply in five-gallon cans, which were the same kind of cans used to hold our gasoline for our vehicles. Now the water cans were painted white on the inside and the gas cans were, of course, painted olive drab. I guess that maybe kept a few idiots from drinking the gasoline

Billy Green and I would go to the water point in the weapons carrier and get fifty or sixty five-gallons cans of water at a time. We would bring the water back to put in a big canvas bag, called a lister bag, which had a little button on the side that you could push and fill your canteen. Then we had to put a certain amount of chlorine tablets in the lister bag to purify the water that we had just poured in.

Charlie Crisa, who was in charge of the "Goon Platoon," came by about that time. (The Goon Platoon was a group of misfits that had messed up at one time or another and were put on KP, digging garbage pits and straddle trenches, and other such manual chores.) Well, Charlie saw us putting the pills in the water, and he wanted to know what they were.

44

I said, "Charlie, that is a military secret, and you didn't see us putting anything in the water."

He said, "Oh, yes you did. I saw you put some little white tablets in the water, and I want to know what they are."

I said, "O.K. I'll go ahead and tell you, but you better promise not to tell a single soul. That's saltpeter tablets that we put in the water bag."

He said, "What?!"

"Yes, that's saltpeter," I told him. "Now, you are over here to fight — not make love. This saltpeter will take care of any of your sexual ambitions or desires, and you'll be like a eunuch."

He said, "Lordy, I knew the army would do a lot of weird things, but I didn't know they would do *that* to a man." He went on off.

In a few minutes, Harry Johnson came by and said, "Hey, Slick. Charlie Crisa said y'all are putting saltpeter in that water. I know what that does to a man."

I said, "Well, Harry, if you are under 30 years old, it will wear off after two or three months and you'll never know it the rest of your life. But if you're over 30, it might just cut you like a steer."

He said, "Damn, I'm 33!" He stomped off, and I watched him as he headed off toward the company area. He stopped Lieutenant Oller and told him, I guess, because I saw Lieutenant Oller slapping his legs and laughing.

Harry then came back by with his carbine on his shoulder, with live ammunition in the chamber. He said, "Slick, you don't have to wait on some German to kill you. Some American is gonna beat 'em to it, and it might just be me!"

I said, "Harry, I was just kidding."

"I know that, Slick," he laughed, and we remained friends from then on.

Green and I had noticed a French house along the way to get the water. As we went back and forth by this house, we had noticed a couple of French girls, and they began to smile and wave at us. I don't remember how they looked, but they were young. Of course, if they had a dress on, they looked pretty good to a soldier.

I was corporal of the guard one night, and I had posted my guards. Green said, "You know the location of all the guard post, so why don't we slip off and go down to see those girls?"

So, about 8:00, we slipped through the lines and went down there. They had a candle burning in the house and invited us in. We had chocolates, chewing gum, cigarettes and such with us. There was an old grandma in there, and she stayed between us and the young girls.

They had some Maribelle, which is sort of like "white lightning." It's made from white apples, and it's about 300 proof — or so it seemed. (They also make cognac and Calvados from those apples.) Green started drinking pretty heavy, and soon he started giggling at everything. I knew that was a bad sign, so I told them all goodbye and we started back to camp.

Green could get drunk quicker than anyone I've ever known, and he was staggering and giggling on the way back. We got back just inside the posted guard area when Green fell. I was carrying a 45 pistol, and he, being a truck driver, carried a Thompson submachine gun. When he fell, he fired a burst from that machine gun, and it nearly scared me to death! Thank God I was behind him or he probably would have blown me away.

Well, then I heard rifle bolts clicking all up and down the line, and people were hollering for the "sergeant of the guard" and "officer of the day," and I never heard such commotion in my life. We kind of eased on in, and I yelled at the nearest guard post to hold his position and that I was on my way.

I got ole Green to his foxhole and then went back out there. The whole company was awake by that time. Down below us was the 300th Signal Battalion, and someone down there fired a couple of rounds. Everyone on guard duty was lined up around the area, standing almost shoulder to shoulder instead of working in shifts. Everyone not on guard duty was ordered to the foxholes. Within 15 minutes, the rumor was spreading that the Germans were dropping paratroopers in behind our line to cut communications. Of course, we couldn't tell them what had really happened or we would have been in major trouble.

Six weeks or so later, I was going down the road in a jeep with Lieutenant Moore. I happened to think about that night and how funny it was—knowing that everyone in the company was wide awake most of the night expecting an invasion, and only Green and I knew the truth.

Well, I started to laugh quietly, and, you know how, when you suppress laughter, it just kind of erupts and explodes like a volcano. Well, Lieutenant Moore said, "What in hell is so funny?" I had to tell him. He threw his helmet down in the jeep and cussed a blue streak, but finally he saw how funny it was.

"The French Barber." T/5 Charles Sumners, 166th Signal Photo Co, U.S. Army Signal Corps (right), strikes the "French Barber pose" before giving victim Cpl. Lou Crabtree a haircut. Trier, Germany, 1945.

The French Barber

The company had a barber named Smith whom we all called Smitty, but he would not be available when we were out in the field for three or four weeks. So I not only was the driver and still photographer, but I also served as a barber.

Corporal Crabtree, about 35 years old, really needed a haircut because his hair had gotten very shaggy. He had black curly hair, and it was neat looking when freshly cut. He had located a barber kit with scissors, comb and hand clippers (worked with your hands—not electricity) for cutting hair.

Crabtree said, "Charlie, you've got to give me a haircut." Before I started cutting, I stood there with the "French Barber pose," and someone took my picture.

I cut his hair and then shaved his neck with the old razor that we found in the barber kit. The razor was rusty, I guess, and I cut him on the neck while I was shaving him. His neck got infected, and we thought it would never get cured. It finally did, but Crabtree and I both had some very anxious moments because his neck looked really bad.

10

ST. MALO

Our unit was following the 83rd Division from the Brest Pennisula on their way to St. Malo. When we headed out, they were well ahead of us and were bypassing a lot of towns along the way. We, however, went into one of those little towns. When the local citizens saw us coming, they knew we were Americans, and they were out in the streets waving and yelling at us.

I did all of the driving, and I noticed this lady standing over on my side of the jeep. She was holding a tumbler and a pitcher full of some white liquid in her hands, and I thought it was white wine. So I stopped, she poured me a little drink and I quickly downed it. Suddenly I felt like someone had put a blowtorch in my mouth — that stuff burned all the way down to my toes!

She ran around to the other side of the jeep, and my mouth was burning so badly that I couldn't say anything. She saw the bars on Lieutenant Moore's uniform, and, realizing he was an officer, poured him about twice the amount she had given me. He liked booze anyway, so he turned it up and gulped down a couple of swigs.

Suddenly he stood up in the jeep and grabbed the windshield. With tears running down his cheeks, he looked down at me and yelled, "What in the Hell was *that*?"

I let out the clutch, and we drove out of that little town with Lieutenant Moore standing up in the jeep with his mouth wide open to let the wind blow in it!

That was our first introduction to Calvados, which is a drink that seems to be about 200 proof alcohol. You could use it for cigarette lighter fluid, or you could light a match to it and have a blue flame. It was so strong it would burn your throat for hours if you didn't dilute it some way.

We then went on to the town of St. Malo where the infantry had gone. The battle was going on there, and we were close enough that we could hear rifle and machine gun fire as well as the burp guns used by the Germans. Shells were going over everywhere, so we decided this was as far as we needed to go. The guys with me asked me to stay with the jeep (in case we needed to get away) while they went on into town to get closer to the action for some photographs of the battle.

I backed the jeep into an alley next to a tall building that had a terra-cotta roof. After about five minutes, the Germans started dropping mortar fire on the roof of that very building, blowing terra-cotta shards down on me, the jeep and all around. I figured it was a matter of time before they laid one of the rounds directly on me.

Cpl. Charles E. Sumners being decorated with the Bronze Star by Col. Hammond of 3rd U.S. Army, June 1945. Wild Bad Kreuth, Bavaria.

When I pulled out into the street, I could go left (back the way we came and out of danger) or I could go right in the direction that Sullivan, Meyer and Moore had gone to take the pictures. Well, I couldn't leave them down there, and I couldn't stay where I was. So, I turned right and headed the jeep down the street toward them. I had gone about one block when one of the infantry lieutenants stepped out of a doorway and asked me, "Where in the hell do you think you are going?"

I saw that my three buddies were pinned down right in the middle of the street behind an old monument that had a little wrought-iron fence around it, and I said to him, "Right down there."

I drove right by this lieutenant and went toward the guys. They saw me as I was circling and made a run for the jeep. Sullivan dived in head first, the others jumped in, and as we left out of there, Sullivan's feet were still sticking up in the air!

We got out of there in a hurry. They were shelling us pretty heavily by that time, and a little further up the road there was an intersection that was under direct machine gun fire. We got two bullet holes in the jeep and a cracked windshield, but —can you believe?— none of us had a single scratch on us!

After the war, I was awarded the Bronze Star for getting those guys out of that mess down there. I am proud of that medal, but I was just trying to save myself and my buddies. I could not have turned left and driven off and left them in those circumstances.

One of the better things about being a photographer was the fact that you could get in, take your pictures, and —if it got too hot —turn tail and run. Many times we had to get out fast, and that's probably one of the reasons we lived through the war.

Bronze Star.

11

AVRANCHES

The town of Avranches in France was one of the larger towns that the Third Army helped liberate after Patton broke out in Normandy and started his mad dash across France. We got to Avranches on August 7, 1944, and we stopped near a boys' school in the town. Several young boys were looking through the fence at the jubilant American soldiers, and we could tell that they were hungry.

When the Germans left Avranches, they carried off all of the foodstuff and stripped everything they could. The people there were obviously hungry, and that disturbed the American soldiers. So the GIs opened their rations and fed the young boys and their families for several days before the food supplies could be brought up to take care of their needs.

I can still see the look of hunger on the faces of the young boys there in that school and the people. They were happy to see us, yet it's hard to be happy when you're hungry. After a few days, the army managed to get supplies up there. Of course, our troops moved on as soon as the town was taken, and we went on through.

One of the young men

An American tank advancing on the road to Avranches. A dead horse and wrecked German equipment can be seen on the roadside. Photograph courtesy of William Peters of *wwii_photos@geocities.com*

French men and boys of Maizieres-Les-Metz, France, stand around fires at the town's garbage and trash dump. Civilians try to salvage food from this dump. U.S. Army Signal Corps; photograph by C.E. Sumners. Stamped: "Confidential. Not to Be Published. Field Press Censor 108."

Reunion at Sofitel Hotel hosted by John F. Lehodey honoring the U.S. 3rd Army in 1994. The 50th Anniversary of the liberation of Avranches, France. Russ Meyer and Charles Sumners. Speaker podium in the background.

in this school that was fed by the soldiers was John F. Lehodey. He grew up to become the president of Hotel Sofitel, a chain of restaurants and hotels in Europe and also in the United States. In June 1994, on the 50th anniversary of the liberation of Avranches, he opened the doors of his Hotel Sofitel North America in Los Angeles to members of the Third Army — free lodging, free everything.

I went to California for this reunion and was joined by eight or ten of my buddies of the 166th Signal Photo Company at the hotel in Los

R O N A L D   R E A G A N

Dear Friends,

I am honored to send my greetings to all those gathered at Hotel Sofitel's commemoration of the fiftieth anniversary of the World War II landings on the beaches of Normandy.

I can hardly believe fifty years have passed since that crisp morning on the 6th of June, when the boys of the allied nations joined together in battle to liberate Europe. Those young men courageously faced their mission -- a mission which would end a blood-curdling war and restore independence.

As our soldiers stormed the white sand beaches, they could see the jagged edge cliffs that lay before them. What thoughts must have been running through their heads! But their commitment to uphold the ideals of democracy and human rights which our forefathers envisioned for us pressed them to move forward to scale those ominous rocks.

A decade ago, I stood on those very rocks -- those wind swept cliffs of Normandy -- as a deep sense of emotion and pride filled my heart with the thought of those determined soldiers who sacrificed their lives in the name of peace. Their mission dramatically changed the course of history and they are clearly revered today as the true champions of freedom -- the dauntless heroes of the ages. It is their faith and undying loyalty to which we owe our yesterdays, todays, and tomorrows.

It is my hope that we will always remember that for which those brave soldiers fought valiantly for and yes, died for, on that cool June morning. There were many survivors -- many of whom are with you today. There were so many others who deserve our deepest respect and our eternal gratitude for sacrificing their lives in the name of lasting peace.

-2-

Let us make an oath to labor together to preserve the legacy of peace and prosperity which was handed to us fifty years ago by those who truly forged freedom's path.

God bless each of you as you remember. May we never forget.

Sincerely,

Ronald Reagan

Letter from President Ronald Reagan to veterans of 3rd Army, World War II.

Angeles. There we saw hundreds of former Third Army veterans. After a couple of people spoke, the mike was left open for anyone to speak. It was primarily used by people trying to locate members of their unit. You'd see some one go up there and say, "I'm looking for 'so and so' Battalion, Company B." Then you'd hear someone yell from the back, and two old men who hadn't seen each other since the war would greet each with a feeling that it was "only yesterday" that they had last said goodbye.

We had a wonderful time there. They collected souvenirs of anything you wanted to put into a time capsule to be opened in another fifty years, on the 100th anniversary of the liberation. Our group gave them a book—*Patton's GI Photographers*, edited by Ralph Butterfield—and all the guys there had a story, a picture or something in the book. We all signed the book, which would be placed along with the other items that other soldiers gave to be placed in the capsule.

They sent us a letter signed by as many of the young men of this school as they could find still alive. On top of it was a picture of a hand. It said, "Merci (Thank you). Thank you for feeding us and helping us in our hour of need."

So it was quite a reunion. The young man had remembered the kindness of the American soldiers those fifty years ago, and this was his way of saying "thank you for caring."

12

PARIS

In August 1944 the American troops were within 25 or 30 miles of Paris and could have taken the city easily. Most of the Germans had already withdrawn from Paris, and they had left only a token German force to defend the city. However, for many reasons, the leaders of the Allied forces decided that American troops should wait for the Second French Armored Division to fight its way up and be the first forces to go in to liberate Paris. General Leclerc was in charge of the division, which American troops had trained down in Africa.

There were two or three chief French political groups vying for supremacy. The Allies wanted the leader of the Free French, General de Gaulle, to be the man in control of France since it was felt that the others would not be as easy to work with after the war was over. So, to give Leclerc and de Gaulle enough time to achieve their objectives, for about 1½ weeks, we were held up from advancing forward.

During this time, my group was waiting in the town of Rambouillet, some 30 miles from Paris. There were many photographers and war correspondents waiting to photograph and write about this big event. Our photo unit, consisting of Lieutenant Moore, Russ Meyer, Charles Sullivan and myself, was probably the only American troop unit in this town. We were there with Bob Capa, the quintessential war correspondent; Ernest Hemingway and Ernie Pyle, both well-known war correspondents; as well as Andy Rooney, correspondent for the *Stars and Stripes*. Of course, we were all waiting for the Second French Armored to get in position to take Paris.

There were really no Germans anywhere near Rambouillet, but Hemingway had a group of the Free French soldiers that he would send out on patrol each day to contact the enemy and gather information for him to be able to write his column. They would come back in and report to Hemingway, and he would send them out again the next day. Each night they would have a big drinking party there in the Hôtel du Grand Veneur, and he would get "soused up."

Hôtel du Grand Veneur. Rambouillet, France. Approximately 30 miles from Paris. Where Ernest Hemingway and his "band of French Maquis holed up" before the liberation of Paris. This photograph taken in 1977 on a trip back to France.

Hemingway had taken over the hotel and had stored hundreds of guns and other weapons in many of the rooms. He sent word to our unit that he was sorry we were having to stay in tents behind the hotel, and offered to compensate us by getting us "first class" treatment with some of his "lady friends." He was a boisterous, vulgar, arrogant, overbearing man, and I didn't like him at all. He was certainly *not* one of my favorite war correspondents.

One of the nicest people that I met during the war was a British correspondent, and he did not like Hemingway either. He and I became good friends and talked daily about the war and other problems. He was a fine man, and we both agreed that Papa Hemingway was an uncouth idiot although he was a very gifted writer and wrote several great books.

Our group from Rambouillet was among the first Americans into Paris. When the Second French Armored Division came in that morning of August 25, 1944, they entered with tanks wide open, waving their flags and yelling "Vive la France!" Charles Sullivan, Russ Meyer, and I fell in with the tank outfit and headed into Paris on the Porte d'Orléans road.

The street was completely lined with people, leaving just enough room for the tanks and the convoy to get through. German snipers were still shooting out of buildings, and this would hold up the convoy from time to time, while soldiers cleared out these sniper nests. It was surprising that this sniper fire did not kill more civilians, because people were as crowded as they could be up and down the street for miles and miles and miles—waving their flags and yelling.

Liberation of Paris, 1944. The crowd at the Place de l'Opéra after the taking of the Kommandantur. Postcard (c. 1944) from Sumners' collection. Edition o.p.— Diffusé par Photo-Presse-Libération 1944.

Liberation of Paris, 1944. General Leclerc's troops parade in the Rue de Rivoli. Postcard (c. 1944) from Sumners' collection. Edition o.p.— Diffusé par Photo-Presse-Libération 1944.

Liberation of Paris, 1944. American tanks in front of the Grand Palais. Postcard (c. 1944) from Sumners' collection. Edition o.p.— Diffusé par Photo-Presse-Libération 1944.

Liberation of Paris, 1944. French girls welcome American troops. Postcard (c. 1944) from Sumners' collection. Edition o.p.— Diffusé par Photo-Presse-Libération 1944.

This entrance into Paris was an experience that I will never forget. Once the French people found out we were Americans, they wanted to get into the jeep with us and shake our hands, hug us, kiss us and pat us on the back. So many of the pretty girls got in the jeep with us that Meyer, with his movie camera, had to ride on the hood of the jeep to take his pictures.

Sullivan was shooting still pictures, and Russ was sitting on the windshield that was lying down on the hood. As he slid down over the hood, the little knob on the windshield snagged and ripped a huge hole in the seat of his pants. Meyer walked around the streets of Paris with some of the French girls goosing him and laughing about it.

Finally he got tired of that, and he was able to get a French Moroccan to sew up his pants—while he was still wearing them, right there on the sidewalk of Paris! It was a sight to see—watching Meyer lying on the hood of the jeep with this fellow sewing up his pants. That would have made a great picture, but I did not take it.

We began to run into heavy rifle fire from the buildings, so I decided to pull the jeep out of this convoy away from the battle scene. I pulled into a courtyard, and suddenly a Frenchman jumped in front of my jeep. I slammed on the brakes, and he was yelling in English, "Stop! Stop!" He then said, "For God's sake, don't go in there. It is heavily mined!"

We could see that the Germans had mined the place and had not had time to camouflage them. We could still see the loose dirt where they had dug the hole to plant

Liberation of Paris, 1944. German prisoner carried away by the Free French. Postcard (c. 1944) from Sumners' collection. Edition o.p.—Diffusé par Photo-Presse-Libération 1944.

Bill Teas.

Free French soldiers arrest a French collaborator for harboring German snipers. French news photographer on right. Dead Germans on steps. Photograph by Bill Teas.

the mines. So, the old Frenchman that spoke English probably saved our lives. He said, "I speak a little English" and told us that he had been reading so he could learn more English words. He showed me the book he was reading, and, to my amazement, it was *The Last of the Mohicans*.

It is very difficult to describe the liberation of Paris. The feelings expressed by those French people as they were being liberated by their own were something to see. The Free French soldiers were going into buildings and dragging out the few Germans left there to the cheers of the French. Most of the German troops had withdrawn by this time, so Paris was spared from a big battle scene that would have destroyed this beautiful old city.

The Free French had cleaned out most of the German sniper nests that remained. They would chase the snipers down the street, and they gathered up the men and women that had collaborated with the Germans. They would beat up the men and kick them; but they would tear the women's clothes, punch them in the face, spit on them and paint their faces with lipstick. They would shave or cut off the women's hair really short, identifying them for several weeks as collaborators.

We had gone all the way into Paris by afternoon, and then had to get our film into the message center for it to be sent back to Army Pictorial Services. We went to a large hotel, which was the headquarters, and I was waiting outside. Suddenly I looked around, and there was a long line of people by my jeep. There were possibly 25 to 30 men, women and kids there, and they started to kiss me. What a scene it was—more kisses than I had ever had in my life. I knew very little French, so I did not understand what they were saying. But I did understand that they were showing their appreciation to an American for helping to liberate their city.

That was quite an experience and one I'll never forget.

That night we met a beautiful lady named Mrs. Suthro who invited us to spend the night with her family. She had a son about 13 years old, and her husband was an officer in the Free French army. We took a bath—the first one in quiet a while and the water was cold—and went to bed on clean sheets. That was the first soft bed we had slept on in a long time.

Soon after we had gone to bed, the Germans sent over some planes and dropped a few bombs on the city. The air raid alarms sounded, and everyone ran to the shelters— everyone except Russ and myself. We decided that we were not going to leave our good beds, no matter what. I thought, "I might get blown out of this bed, but I'm going to stay." As it turned out, the raid did not amount to much, and we had a great night's rest.

The next day we were by the Arc de Triomphe and watched General de Gaulle lead the Second French Armored Division in the victory parade down the Champs Elysées to Notre Dame Cathedral.

With General de Gaulle was General Jacques-Philippe Leclerc, second in command of the Second French Army. I went up to make a picture of General Leclerc. He rapped me on the head with his riding crop and said to an interpreter, "Tell that soldier that General Leclerc allows no one to take his picture without his permission."

Liberation of Paris, 1944. The Free French Forces parading through the Place de la Concorde. Postcard (c. 1944) from Sumners' collection. Edition o.p.—Diffusé par Photo-Presse-Libération 1944.

He was standing there in a uniform that American money had paid for. All of his equipment and everything used by the Second French Armored Division was GI. And he is telling me that I can't take his picture. I didn't take his picture. Later he told the interpreter that he would allow me to take his picture. By then I had decided that I didn't *want* to take his picture. I turned my back to him and left them standing there.

On the 29th, we watched the U.S. 28th Infantry Division march down the Champs Elysées. This parade let the Parisians know that the American troops were also there to protect them. That day, the cry from the crowd was "Vive l'Américain!"

Liberation of Paris, 1944. American troops (28th Infantry) parade in the Champs-Elysées. Postcard (c. 1944) from Sumners' collection. Edition o.p. — Diffusé par Photo-Presse-Libération 1944.

Russ Meyer and I have visited Paris many times since the end of World War II. It is a beautiful city with many modern buildings, but much of it is still old like the buildings we saw during the war. Riding the metro on one of these visits brought back happy memories of the subway during those earlier days.

During the war, riding the metro was free for anyone wearing an American, British, Canadian or French uniform. It was a wonderful way to get around Paris, and you could get to almost any part of the city using this system. They had weddings, birthday parties, champagne parties and festivities of all kinds on the metro.

We had a few days in Paris after the liberation before we had to move on. These were fun times in a happy atmosphere. The French people in Paris treated us like royalty, and we enjoyed every minute of it. I can still see those crowds lining the streets — laughing and crying while waving American and French flags. I suppose being there for the liberation of Paris was the highlight of all the things that happened to me during World War II.

Paris on R & R

You could only send home just so much money, so we would save up a good bit of money from selling German souvenirs. When we got a break from combat, I would go into Paris on a three-day pass, with two or three hundred dollars, and, before I could spit, I would be broke again.

Charles Sumners with Eiffel Tower in background. On three-day pass to Paris, France, April 1945. Photograph by Lou Crabtree.

In front of Arc de Triomphe, Paris, France. May 4, 1945. Charles Sumners and Lou Crabtree.

Once, I went into Paris by myself, and I got lost while trying to find a certain bar. I could see light at the other end of this dark alley, so I started walking toward it. I was about halfway through when three kids that looked about 16 to 17 years old came out of a doorway and started after me. I started walking faster and faster, looking back over my shoulder. I was getting ready to run, but, when I looked up, in front of me were some more.

I had heard stories about people being mugged, robbed and left wearing only their underwear; sometimes they were beaten up or killed. I figured that this was about to happen to me because I didn't have a pistol or any other type of weapon with me.

Before they got to me, however, a man came out of a doorway and said something in French to these boys, but I didn't know enough French to know what he said. He must have said that he

Soldiers enjoy a sidewalk café while in Paris on three-day pass, April 1945. Charles Sumners and Lou Crabtree.

had a gun and for them to leave me alone, because they turned and headed back to where they had come from.

The guy then came and told me, in English, "You almost got yourself in a mess, didn't you soldier?"

I told him, "Yes, sir" and remarked about his speaking English.

He told me that he had been born in France but had gone to the United States before the war. He figured the only way to get back to France was to join the army. When his outfit got close to Paris after the city was liberated, he came back to the area where he was born and raised. He changed from uniform to civilian clothes and was presently working as a bartender. As he put it, "Since I know how to speak French, I am now a Frenchman again."

I told him that I was glad he was there at that alley that night to help me. We then went on down to the bar where he worked. I saw him two or three times later because I would make a point to go by and see him on trips back to Paris.

I owed him quite a bit, as I easily could have been killed that night or hurt badly at best. I did not take any more short cuts in Paris on future visits. I had learned the danger of such moves, and I made sure to stay out in areas where there was plenty of light and lots of people.

13

REIMS

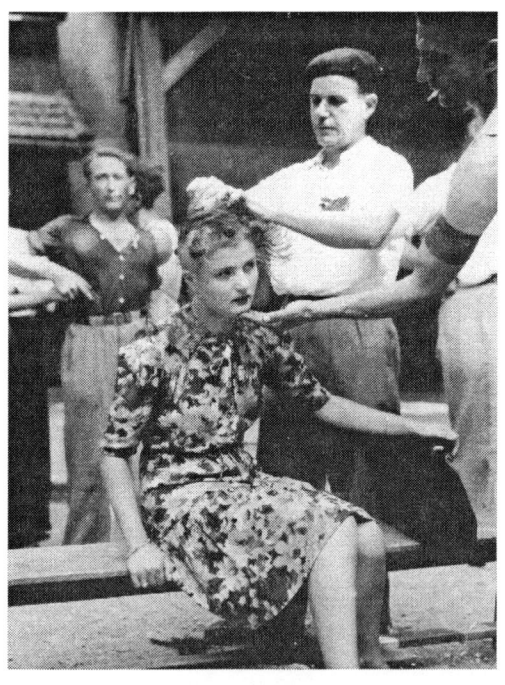

This girl pays the penalty for having had personal relations with the Germans. Here, in the Montelimar area, France, French civilians shave her head as punishment. Smith, August 29, 1944. National Archives at College Park, MD.

We were with the Seventh Armored Division that took the town of Reims and had some interesting experiences then. We had another photo unit, the 167, working with us. Bill Miller, a good-looking soldier from one of the Northern states, was sitting in my jeep smoking a cigar. Suddenly a very nice-looking French girl jumped in the jeep, took the cigar out of his mouth and put it in her mouth. Then she put her arms around his neck, and he was thrilled to death with that move.

I noticed a group of very angry people approaching us and wondered what was going on. They reached in, jerked her out of the jeep and proceeded to cut off all her hair. Then they painted her all over with lipstick and tore off half of her clothes. We thought they were going to kill her, so we pulled our guns out and made them turn her loose. She hurried down the street looking back over her shoulder.

I don't know what happened to her, but it sure took the wind out of Bill's sails. We found out later that she had been married to a Frenchman and had a couple of

Champagne Pommery & Greno — Reims, 1944. Junction of two galleries and views of the carrier system. Postcard (c. 1945) from Sumners' collection. (Permission granted by Champagne Pommery & Greno.)

kids, but she had taken up with a German soldier. This was the way the French people treated "collaborators" like her.

That night in Reims, we went down to the Pommery Champagne Distillery. We saw miles of tunnels under the ground with thousands of bottles of champagne. They gave us two cases of this great stuff—wrapped in the straw—for six of us that were staying in the hotel that night.

We began to drink the champagne, and the next morning several guys started shaking the empty bottles to see if they could find a drop or two left in any of them. We had consumed the whole 24 bottles of champagne that night. I was

Left: The Cathedral of Reims, 1944. Postcard (c. 1945) from Sumners' collection. (Permission granted by Champagne Pommery & Greno.)

never a heavy drinker and didn't drink very much that night. But Lieutenant Moore did drink possibly the most of anyone, and he had dysentery for the next few days. We made many stops for him to head to the bushes to relieve himself.

Reims was a beautiful town with a magnificent cathedral, but it was put off limits to the soldiers a few days after it was liberated.

14

NANCY, FRANCE—THE BIG GUN

When you think of war, you think of guns of all types—rifles, pistols, machine guns and field artillery pieces. Probably the largest guns in the war were like the guns at Navarone, but among the largest were the German railway guns that were mounted on railroad flat cars and pulled from place to place. They also had another large gun that they would mount on two Tiger tanks—one in the front and one in the rear—which would transport the guns to locations where they could not have been taken by railway.

The Third Army had set up headquarters in Nancy, France, and the town was being shelled constantly by one of these big guns, which was located somewhere outside the town. They had tried aerial photos and every method they could think of to find this gun but had not been able to locate it. The gun was so big that it had the capability of firing a distance of 30 to 40 miles, so it was no easy task to pinpoint its location.

Finally, a group from Signal Radio Intelligence was sent in and given the task of finding it. Russ Meyer and I were back at Cheligny, which was not too far from Nancy, so we were given the job of photographing this task force at work.

The radio equipment being used was located in a trailer and it was really packed tight in there. Meyer was working his movie camera to capture this event, and I was assigned to write captions about something that I knew nothing about. I would help Russ move his tripod around and keep his film supply handy, but I was not authorized to take any still shots.

This signal outfit was able to pinpoint the location of the gun by sound waves, and soon the air force was able to bomb it and put it out of commission. It had been in a cave some 30 miles from Nancy and was mounted on railroad tracks. The Germans would use a small engine to push the big gun outside the cave on those tracks, and, after firing off a round, they would run it back inside the cave and close the door. They had the door so well camouflaged that it would not show up in any aerial photographs.

The barrel on some of these big guns like the CMK5 was 70 feet long and the shell

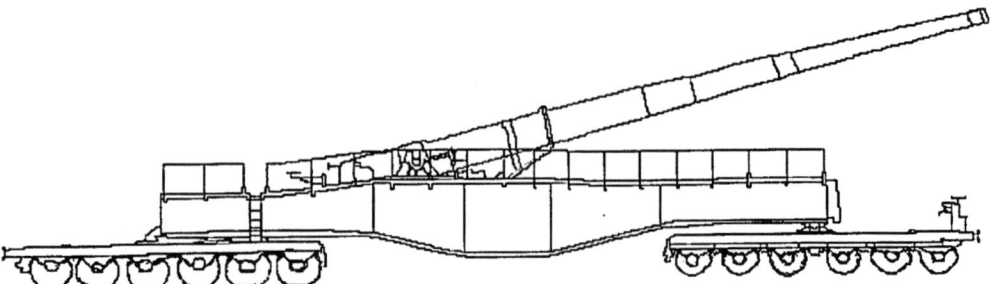

Drawing of "Big Railway Gun." These huge guns were mounted on railcars and rolled out from camouflaged tunnels when being fired. Drawing by Mark Sumners.

weighed as much as 662 pounds. The big gun at Nancy possibly was not able to fire rounds quite that large, but they were really big rounds and would do a considerable amount of damage. I saw a piece of shrapnel from one of the shells that weighed around 25 pounds, and it had gone through four buildings, finally landing in the floor of a barbershop. A lot of people went by to see this because we had never heard of a piece of shrapnel that large before.

Of course, this had been a very secret job to do for this signal outfit with their radio equipment. The job was so secret that the army sent special agents to check into Russ Meyer's background since he was the one making the pictures. The possible reason for the background check was that his parents were originally from Germany. His mother wrote and asked him what he had done and why all these people were coming to California asking questions about him. They didn't bother to check on this ole Alabama farm boy, as far as I ever knew.

We did receive a letter of commendation from the War Department for our part in taking pictures of this operation. Of course, we didn't have anything to do with locating the gun. We were just there four or five days taking pictures of the operation and all the radio equipment used to locate the big gun.

The Germans had used some of these huge guns on the Russian front at the Battles of Leningrad and Stalingrad. In fact, just about any place you saw the German Army, they would usually have some of those big railroad guns close by. They had them along the coastline in France at Navarone and other towns along the coastline.

One of the big disadvantages of most of these big guns was the fact that they could not maneuver to turn the full 360° around to fire at all locations. They would only go so far, so you could get around their limited mobility area and not be hit by their shells.

The Germans' big Elephant tanks also had big guns that would shoot large shells for greater damage to a target, but their guns would not turn the full 360° as would the guns on the American tanks. So, even though our tanks did not have such fire power, we were much more mobile and could use that to our advantage in a firefight with the German tanks. Those Elephant tanks always went in pairs and would set up rear to rear so one could protect the backside of the other.

15

CHELIGNY

For a while, our company headquarters was located in Cheligny, and we had rooms up over a billiard parlor about 200 yards up the hill from where the rest of the company was located. In Cheligny, sleeping quarters of most buildings were upstairs, and many houses were built over the families' stables or cattle stalls.

The most amazing thing would happen every morning. A little boy would come up the hill wearing a little hat that had a feather in it, and he blew a little horn several times as he came up through the town. All the sheep, goats and cows would come out into the street, fall in behind him and follow him up to the mountain pasture to graze all day. If someone were late with their milking when the horn blew, that old cow would still come out of the stable and fall in behind the young boy with the horn.

In the afternoon, they would come back down from the mountain. When each animal got to its barn or stable, it would peel off from the group and go into its own stall. I thought it was the most amazing thing to see, and everyday I would go out and watch this scene take place.

Ted Covalence was a member of the company, and he was a gate guard who was on duty every night of the week. He was always there with his old mackinaw turned up over his ears with a carbine rifle slung on his shoulder. Willie Breedlove

Street scene in Cheligny, France. The building in center was location of the billiard parlor and pub over which some members of the 166th soldiers lived. Photograph by C.E. Sumners, who wrote on the back, "Town not pretty, but the girls were cute."

The billiard parlor in Cheligny, France. Above were rooms where soldiers stayed.
Homer Foreman and Mike Furduska.

Cheligny, France. The boy collected all the sheep, goats, cows, and so on, in the town
and led them to pasture until end of day. Each animal instinctively went to its home
each evening as they returned. Photograph by C.E. Sumners, 1945.

and I had an old flare pistol that would make flares. There was a gate coming into the area where we were living, and Ted was always there by the gate. So Breedlove and I slipped down there behind the wall by the lab trailer one midnight and took that old flare pistol and shot it up right over Covalence's head. It got his attention very quickly, and I have never heard so much yelling in my life. He woke up the whole company. In the meantime Breedlove and I slipped on up behind the wall to where we were staying and went to bed.

The next day, you have never heard the amount of wild stories that floated around about what happened the night before. They said it was an air raid, and Ted said he saw them drop that flare out of the airplane. He said that he could even see the belly of the plane as it flew on off and that the plane did not drop any bombs, although he was expecting one to be dropped any minute.

Of course, we didn't tell them anything different.

Another memory of days in Cheligny comes to mind. Harry Johnson from Griffin, Georgia, was in our company and had an air mattress. Every night he would take it up to the motor pool, inflate it, then put it on his bed under his blankets and sleep on it. He carried this air mattress all the way from Camp Crowder in Missouri to Ireland, then to England and into France.

"Little Willie" Grogan. Fort Driant, France, 1944, wearing a Mackinaw. His real name was Willie Breedlove, and he had told a girl at Camp Crowder that his name was Grogan. He continuously got letters addressed to Willie Grogan, and everyone called him "Little Willie" Grogan.

Finally someone ratted on him to the executive officer, Lieutenant Hunter, about his air mattress. So he was told to bring the air mattress down behind the mess hall. Lieutenant Hunter took his riding crop and used it to draw on the ground a 6 by 6 by 6 (6' wide, 6' long, and 6' deep hole). He instructed Harry to dig this and told him, "Then you'll put your air mattress down there, and then you'll fill in the hole to cover it up."

So every afternoon when Harry got through with his regular duties, he would go out there and dig some more on his hole. Harry didn't care much for manual labor at all, so Lagnell, one of the cooks in the mess hall who was a friend of Harry's, decided he would help ole Harry dig. So he got in the hole digging and shoveling.

About that time Lieutenant Hunter happened to come by and saw him and said, "Lagnell, what are you doing down in there?"

Lagnell replied, "Well you know how it is, Sir. You don't get enough work in the mess hall cooking, so I thought I would just get in this hole and get some exercise by digging."

Lieutenant Hunter replied, "Come on out of that hole and come over here with me."

T/5 Charles Sumners, 166th Signal Photo Co., U.S. Army Signal Corps, wearing German helmet and trench coat to pose for picture of "Flash" Jones — "capturing a German!" Soldier on left is "Flash" Jones. Conflans, France, Sept. 1944.

Lieutenant Hunter then did the same thing he had done with Harry. He marked off a 6 by 6 by 6 and told Lagnell, "Now, this is yours. The other spot you were digging in belongs to Harry, and he doesn't need any help with his."

16

FORT DRIANT

Fort Driant was just across the Moselle River. It was not too far from Metz and was known as the Fortress of Metz. It had never been and never was taken by frontal assault, and General Patton had said he would "take it or they would haul the dogtags back in 2½-ton trucks." Our troops of the Fifth Division tried to take it for several days, maybe a week or more, and casualties ran high. Finally, by October 9, Patton listened to cooler heads and bypassed it.

The fort was actually just a mountainside full of tunnels, and they could seal off sections of those tunnels. If you managed to blow the door open and take one section, they could just seal it off and you had nowhere to go. So it was difficult to try to take it in the first place.

We had bombed it, shelled it, and done everything to it; but it went deep into the mountainside and was fortified with cement and steel. There were huge rooms, sleeping quarters, mess halls and all kinds of rooms for activities of every kind you could think of.

A few weeks after we bypassed Fort Driant, the few Germans who were still there surrendered because they ran out of food. We went back to photograph the official surrender.

Some of my buddies and I went back there two or three times after the war, but we were unable to get into Fort Driant. The

Willy Breedlove wearing Lt. Moore's trench-coat, riding a German motorbike after surrender of Germans at Fort Driant. He wrecked the bike and ruined the coat a few yards down the road. 1944. Photograph by C.E. Sumners.

French army is now using it for training purposes, and it would have been quite a job going through channels to get permission to visit it.

On the other side of the river from Fort Driant was the town of Maizieres-les-Metz. The battalions of the 90th Division tried for several days to take the town, but German artillery — the guns they had there in Fort Driant — was formidable. The Germans had used the countryside and surrounding area in training and knew everything about it, so assaulting the town proved very difficult. We finally had to bypass Metz and go down below to cross the Moselle River.

I went across the river one night with a patrol — I really don't know why. But we got across the river and moved on up to a ridge above the river. There were about ten of us with a lieutenant and a sergeant. The lieutenant told us to quietly dig foxholes, so we started and slowly dug out foxholes big enough to get down into without being seen.

When the sun came up the next morning, we could see German soldiers, about 150 yards away. They were cooking breakfast on what looked like little old stoves — steel ranges of some kind. We could hear them talking even though we couldn't understand what they were saying. We didn't know what to do, but we couldn't talk above a whisper, and we had to stay down in the foxholes all day. The lieutenant said we should take everything out of our pockets and bury it in the bottom of our foxholes, keeping only our dogtags. That was in case we were captured.

155mm artillery firing on Fort Driant near Metz, France. U.S. Army Signal Corps; photograph by C.E. Sumners. Stamped: "Confidential, Until Reclassified by Censor."

River covered with smoke. Outpost on Moselle River. Fort Driant is across the river. U.S. Army Signal Corps; photograph by C.E. Sumners. Stamped: "Confidential, Until Reclassified by Censor."

Some of us had something to eat, but we didn't get up or move around or move out. I didn't take any pictures because that would have required getting up, and getting pictures was *not* the most important thing to me at that time!

Luckily, the Germans moved back and we never knew why. Our artillery was shelling over us, and that might have been the reason. We could see the artillery hitting around and below them. Anyway, they moved back, but that day was the longest day that I have ever spent. That night, as soon as it got dark, we moved back down to the river. We contacted the people on the other side, and they sent two rafts back across to pick us up.

We all got back safe and sound, and I got back without a picture. That was my last night patrol. I had had all of that that I wanted!

For a while during November 1944, we were living not too far from Metz. Mike Marder, another still photographer, had joined our outfit. Lieutenant Moore, Meyer and Mike decided to go into town one day, supposedly to see the library, museum and such. They asked me to go, but I told them "no thanks." I knew that they were headed into town to a house of ill repute, and I didn't want to go. Besides, a little old lady up the street was going to show me how to catch some fish, even though snow was on the ground up to your knees.

As they left Metz driving back, the streets were icy and slick. Mike was driving and ran by the place to turn off. Lieutenant Moore yelled at him, and Mike, not being used to such road conditions, slammed on the brakes. The jeep flipped upside down, throwing Mike and Lieutenant Moore out. The jeep then turned upside down on top of Meyer.

Russ had a pretty good lick on the head and would pass out from time to time. Finally an ambulance got there and loaded them up. While they were getting Meyer from under the jeep, he discovered that someone had stolen his watch — apparently while he was passed out. He got mad and would not get in the ambulance with the other two.

He refused to go to the hospital, insisting that he was all right. So he got someone to bring him back to where we were living. The next morning his knee was so swollen that it looked like a basketball and was black as it could be. It was bruised badly, and he could not bear to walk on it.

Lieutenant Moore and Mike were released from the hospital in about three weeks, but, meanwhile, I was having to tear up this old house making firewood to keep Meyer warm. I had to get his food for him also, and I would get as much food as the cooks would allow me to take to him. Regardless, every time I took him his food, he would always say the same thing: "Is that all you got?"

"Slick" Sumners breaking up furniture for firewood in house near Metz, France, 1944.

Russ Meyer in house near Metz, France, 1944. Meyer's knee was injured when his jeep over-turned. Photograph by C.E. Sumners.

This place did not have indoor plumbing — just an outhouse. Russ had a chamber pot to use since he couldn't walk on that leg, and I had to empty it each day. Later, I could get him up and let him lean on me to get out to the outhouse to do his business. I would leave him for a little while, and then I would hear him yell, "SUM-NERS!" It was cold as blue blazes at that time, and I would wait a few more minutes before I went to get him. I would hear him yell louder, "Sum-NERS!" I would finally go out to get him, and he would be about frozen stiff. I'd make out like I hadn't heard him the first go, but he didn't believe this at all.

By this time, I had burned up chairs, beds, a dresser, and about anything else I could find to use as firewood to keep us from freezing to death. I had burned up every stick of furniture in that house except one chair and the bed that Russ was sleeping in. Lieutenant Moore came finally to tell us that he had secured another jeep and that we had an assignment to go to the Tenth Armored Division.

Russ said he was ready to go, but his knee still looked awful. They still wanted him to go to the hospital to check on it, but he refused to go. So, we loaded up the jeep and headed out to the new assignment.

We tried to find this place again when Russ, Gene Abrams and I were back there after the war, but it had been so long that we were unable to locate it. Perhaps, later on, the rest of this old house had been destroyed and used for firewood also.

17

Belgium and "The Bulge"

On December 15, 1944, somewhere in Belgium, Lieutenant Moore, Sergeant Meyer and I decided we had had enough combat for a while. We had been in every major campaign or battle since we had left the beaches. So we decided we would spend Christmas week in Paris. We left early on the 15th and drove nonstop to reach Paris on the afternoon of the 16th. When we got to Paris, we were told that the Germans had started a major offensive push in the Ardennes Forest and were pushing our lines back. Of course, we were ordered back to the front.

On our way back to the front, we went through the little town of Conflans-Jarney, near Verdun, and stopped to stay with the Uriet family. We had rented rooms from them once before when we had been assigned to the 20th Corps and decided to stop by to see them again.

They were happy to see us. They had two little boys—Ramon and Gilbert—and a little girl named Susan who was about 13 years old. I guess because of my small size and young boyish looks, this little girl had a crush on me.

That afternoon while I was standing outside, a very pretty brunette girl walked by. She smiled and waved to me, so I walked out and took her hand and walked down to the end of the block with her and turned to walk back. When I got back, Susan fussed at me in French, then said something to a little French boy that she had gone to find. The little boy could speak English, and he said to me, "Susan says you are not to walk with that mademoiselle because she has a week-old baby by a German soldier."

Well, that stopped my promenading.

We had GI rations that consisted of one-gallon cans of bacon and all such types of food. Mrs. Uriet fried up a couple of pans of the bacon with waffles and orange marmalade. After a good meal and saying our good-byes, we headed on toward the front.

We made it back all right — to the Belgium town of St. Hubert — and joined an infantry company in a three-story building that had windows along the sides facing the Germans.

79

You could look down into the courtyard about 150 yards away and see the German positions, and, once in a while, they would dart from one place to the other.

Infantrymen in Belgium. 1944. National Archives. Courtesy of Stephen Payne of *paynes@ alleg.edu http://webpub.alleg.edu/student/p/paynes/war.html*

Neither side was firing on the other at that time, and Meyer wanted to shoot some footage. He said to one of the infantrymen at the window, "Why don't you fire several rounds at them. I'll get behind you and get a shot of you firing out the window, and then I'll get out my telephoto lens and get a shot of the Germans firing back at this building."

Well, if you pointed a camera at any GI, he automatically thought he was in the movies, and he'd do whatever you asked him to do. So, this guy opened up firing a number of rounds, and Russ made pictures with the normal lens. He was in the process of getting out his telephoto lens when a sergeant came up from downstairs and asked them, "What in the hell is going on up here?"

When he saw the camera, he said to us, "You guys get out of here. We have been here for four hours, and it's the first rest we have had in days. You guys come in here and mess it up, and now we've got the war on again!"

Some of the soldiers had been sitting around taking a break, eating, smoking and some were even sleeping — until we arrived. It didn't take us long to get out of there.

The best part of our job was that we could leave at any time the situation got too hot for us, but, of course, the infantrymen had to stay and carry on the fighting. One of the reasons many of the combat photographers lived through the war was the fact that we *could* bail out if the action got too bad.

Lieutenant Moore was my unit officer and he was a good man. He said many times that he had two goals. Number one was to get the best combat pictures that we could possibly make, and the next goal was to see that all of his men lived through the war.

We did get some very good combat pictures, and Russ Meyer had some of the best combat movie photos of anyone in the company or, for that matter, of anyone in Europe. We also had quite a few excellent still photographers, but not too many people wanted to work with Russ and me. They would say, "You two people are crazy. You are going to get killed, and we don't want any part of you."

So, before the war was over, it was just Meyer and I working together, and I was not going to let him make a coward of me. Someone had to go with him or he would have taken pictures until some German shot him. I pulled him out of quite a few scrapes, and later on he would thank me. He told many of the others that I had saved his ass many times, and that he was alive today because of me.

He never forgot and has been very good to me, and my family, through the years. He and I have shared some bad times, and we have shared some good times. We are still good friends today and will remain good friends until we die.

During the Battle of the Bulge, my feet were frozen and were hurting something awful. I decided to check into an aid station and possibly go to a hospital to get them checked out. Sergeant Meyer and Lieutenant Moore waited outside for me to see what the doctors were going to tell me.

I took off my shoes and socks, and lay down on a cot to wait for the doctor. I had been in there about 15 minutes when a doctor came in and said, "Everyone who is able to walk get up and get out of here. The Germans are only three or four miles away. They are advancing, and we are evacuating this area."

Sgt. Russ Meyer. Photograph by C.E. Sumners.

T/5 Charles E. Sumners with Speed Graphic 4×5 camera, 166th Signal Photo Co.

I got up, put my old socks and shoes back on and hobbled back out to the jeep, and we left. Now Meyer's feet were in bad shape also, but he was too stubborn to admit it. I was concerned with getting home safely and being able to walk okay when I did get home.

Later, while we were staying with an old Belgium couple in St. Hubert, the old lady doctored our feet. After a day of shooting film, we would come in half frozen. This old lady would take off our shoes and put our feet in a tub of snow. She would then pour cold water in the foot tub on top, and the feeling would gradually come back to our feet.

She took a GI woolen blanket and made each of us about three pair of sleeve socks, each put on over the other. We would then put our overshoes on over these socks and just lay our boots aside. We were able to wear these old sleeve socks and overshoes for several days.

I have a big toe on one foot and a little toe on the other foot that have very little feeling today. I guess being frozen did something to the circulation. But this old lady probably saved us from losing our toes or feet to frostbite.

Russ and I joined the Second Cavalry Group and thought it would be an excellent opportunity for us to get some pictures of the Germans. I didn't think too much about it, but this group of jeeps and GIs did not have any tanks attached to it. After a couple of days and nights, we were some 15 or 20 miles ahead of any of our crew and behind the German lines.

We had not made a single picture because we had not seen anything to shoot. There

Chow is served to American Infantrymen on their way to La Roche, Belgium. 347th Infantry Regiment. National Archives at College Park, MD; photograph by Newhouse, Jan. 13, 1945.

was no combat taking place, and the enemy was nowhere to be seen. Finally after about 2½ days, we told them that we were wasting our time and that we had better get back to an area where we would be safer. The soldiers told us how to get back, and we headed out sometime that afternoon. They had told us that we had plenty of time to get back to the American lines where we would be safe.

However, we didn't figure on getting lost — but we did. I never was one for directions or following instructions, and I took a wrong turn. It started getting dark, and the weather turned nasty with the wind blowing hard. We spotted an old barn with double doors on the front, so we headed over to it, opened those doors, put our jeep inside and closed the doors. There was no livestock in the barn, and I didn't see a house, so it possibly had been destroyed already.

It was impossible to leave under such weather conditions, so not bothering to get any sleeping bags out, we just lay down on some hay on the barn floor and went to sleep. Now, I could sleep through air raids, artillery barrages and about anything when I was tired and am hard to wake up once I have gone to sleep. Sometime later, Russ woke me up and said that he heard something coming.

We eased up to the front of the barn. It was just getting a little daylight, so we could see a column of troops coming. As they got closer, we could tell they were German. There were two jeeps moving very slowly, with about 20 soldiers walking beside the jeeps.

Deep snow banks on a narrow road halt military traffic in the woods of Wallerode, Belgium.
87th Infantry Division. National Archives at College Park, MD; photograph by Norbuth,
Jan. 30, 1945.

We were scared, but they went on by as the rain continued to fall. They never seemed to
look in our direction at the old barn or check it out at all.

We decided to wait another hour to see if there were some more German troops coming behind them. We had finally opened the doors getting ready to leave when we heard

someone else coming down the road from the same direction the others had come. When we determined that it was American troops with tanks and half-tracks carrying a group of infantrymen, we flagged them.

The lead tank stopped, and a lieutenant stuck his head up and asked us what in the world we were doing there. They had been told that this area was full of Germans. Meyer told the lieutenant, "No, Charlie and I have already run the Germans off and it's safe for you now."

We then told them that we had seen a small group of Germans pass by with two jeeps and no tanks. We told them where we had been and where we had been trying to go. They told us how to get back to our outfit, and then they headed out after the Germans.

Later on that morning, we found G-2 and got in touch with Lieutenant Moore who was worried about us. He had not known where we had been or what we had been doing all this time. But that was par for the course, as he hardly ever did know.

In Belgium I experienced a Christmas I shall never forget. It was in 1944, on a snow-covered hillside during the Battle of the Bulge. We had been kicked about in early battles with the Germans and were unsure about what was going on.

A small group of GIs was gathered around an army chaplain for a Christmas service. So many of the boys listening to this chaplain had been in so many battles, and you could tell by their appearance that war is hell. There were guys with their heads tied up with scarves, or their feet wrapped up in rags. Many had had to sleep and fight and live in their clothes and shoes for days. Many had frozen hands and feet and had not slept or bathed or shaved for a long time. They were all dirty, cold and scared.

I don't remember specifically what the chaplain said that day, but I remember vividly the faces of those young men. Some stood as stoic as zombies while some cried as the chaplain spoke of home, love, Christ, and what Christmas was all about.

As I looked around and saw tears running down the cheeks of many of these infantrymen, I realized that some of them would never see another Christmas. And many did not. They died at Bastogne, St. Hubert, Malmédy and other battlegrounds too numerous to recall.

I made a lot of pictures of combat and of many things, but the picture of these young soldiers on that snow covered hillside at Christmastime exists only in my memory bank. Nevertheless, it is just as vivid and chilling today as it was at that time, and each Christmas I am reminded of that scene — a long way from home for all of us.

During the fighting in the Ardennes, Meyer and I were at the edge of a clearing and could hear firing in the distance that sounded like a tank battle. We looked out across a wide-open expanse of snow and saw two American tanks, one about 200 yards below us and another coming directly toward us. We heard a flash and saw this tank slip around sideways. The tank took a hit, but it did not stop; it kept coming toward us. It then took a direct hit and came to a stop about 25 yards from where we were lying on the ground in hiding.

We saw the turret open; a tanker climbed out, rolled off the side of the tank, and landed on his feet. I started out to him, but Meyer grabbed me by the arm and said, "No — No — Wait." Then he yelled to the soldier, "Over here," and the tanker stumbled toward our direction. He got to within 15 or 20 feet of the woods and fell face up. Russ and I then ran out and grabbed him by the shoulders and dragged him into the woods, leaving a trail of blood in the snow the entire distance.

His body was full of shrapnel, and he was saying, "No, God, not me. Not me, God, not me."

Field artillery men of the 87th division, 8th corps, 3rd U.S. Army, keep warm around fire between missions near Fruex, Belgium. They are using shell casings for fuel. U.S. Army Signal Corps; photograph by C.E. Sumners. Stamped: "Confidential. Passed for Publication as Censored. 10 JAN 1945."

In two or three minutes, he was dead there at our feet. His body was full of shrapnel, from his neck down, and the blood bubbling out of him covered the snow where he lay.

I still remember those words, and they will always be with me: a dying soldier saying, "No, God. Not me. Not me, God, not me."

That is another picture I did not take, but one that is in my memory bank forever.

As I was looking through my album of World War II pictures, I thought of the many things that affect you. You forget the majority, but some you never do. You carry the images with you, always.

When we had left the front lines, there was not much going on. We were with the Ninth Armored, and they were just more or less holding a position. We were trying to find a place to get warm and keep from freezing and getting frostbite on our feet. We did not know at that time that the Germans were getting ready for that "massive offensive" that was to take place in the Ardennes woods.

The Germans had amassed about 250,000 or more of their best troops for this campaign and many of their best Panzer divisions. They had information that would help them to make their push against one of our greenest divisions—one that had been there

Medics helping injured soldier, France, 1944. National Archives at College Park, MD.

only a few weeks. We did not expect this breakout by the Germans, so we did not have many men in reserve at that time. General Eisenhower had some 60 to 65 divisions, but they were scattered over about a 500-mile front. We did not have enough divisions in reserve to get to a trouble spot quickly. So when the Germans hit this green division of American troops, they just blew them out. They were able to roll over them at will. The Germans were able to penetrate some 65 miles or so into our lines over about a 45-mile front.

The 101st Airborne Division was trucked into the town of Bastogne with orders to hold it at all cost, and they did. They held this town for nine days and were under constant attacks by enemy tanks, artillery and infantry, and everything under the sun. They refused to surrender to the Germans, and they held out despite not having our air force to help. The weather was so miserable with fog, rain, sleet and snow that our planes could not get in the air.

We joined the Fourth Armored Division, which had orders from General Eisenhower to General Patton for him to fight through to aid the defenders at Bastogne as quickly as he could. On the January morning that we were on the road several miles from Bastogne, the fog lifted and the snow stopped. The skies opened on this area, and soon you could hear the men in the tanks shouting and yelling with joy. The sky became dark and totally covered with formation after formation of American and British bombers and fighters, and they were coming and going and coming and going all morning long. You could see and hear groups of planes, one after the other, headed toward their targets to bomb the Germans who were trying to take Bastogne.

Sometime a little after noon we broke through. The Germans had tank traps and trees lying across the roads to slow our advance. There was very little left of Bastogne by the time we broke through to the town. It was battered and a lot of the buildings were destroyed. Much of the area was covered with the dead, both German and American. Some of the bodies were lying frozen to the ground, some frozen to their guns. The 101st Airborne Division troops were happy to see us come to their rescue as they were about out of supplies. The fact that our planes were able to bomb and strafe made it possible to whip the Germans.

U.S. soldiers take cover under fire somewhere in Germany. National Archives, courtesy of Franklin D. Roosevelt Library Digital Archives.

After the Battle of the Bulge, we would go 40 or 50 miles a day and meet only token resistance from the German troops. They could have prolonged the war for a good while if they had not lost all their top fighting men and equipment in the offensive. Many German soldiers and some of their best equipment were captured at the end of this battle. They lost enough people and equipment there in the Battle of the Bulge to have made going into Germany a lot rougher than it was.

That big toe on my right foot and the little toe on my left foot remind me of the Battle of the Bulge, and I almost lost all of my toes to the cold weather. My pants would freeze to the side of the jeep while we were in our vehicles on the move at that time. My hands would get so cold that they would get numb, making it hard to drive or to press the button on a camera to take our photographs.

Pvt. Cluster, Ranger, Texas, looks out of foxhole in snow-covered field near Fruex, Belgium. He was with a field artillery battalion of the 87th division, 3rd Army. Part of artillery unit is camped in tents in background. U.S. Army Signal Corps; photograph by C.E. Sumners. Stamped: "Confidential. Passed for Publication as Censored. 10 JAN 1945."

Most of the pictures that I made in Paris and in the Battle of the Bulge are lost. I tried to mail the prints home, and they never got home. Most of the combat pictures that I have were made after the Bulge. I have only three of the photos that were made in the Ardennes snow.

We came back from the Ardennes area and went to the town of Metz in late January 1945. After a short time in Luxembourg, we then joined the Tenth Armored Division and started out again.

18

SAAR-MOSELLE TRIANGLE

In February 1945, following a short rest after the Bulge, men and tanks of the Tenth Armored Division returned to the front and helped clear the Saar-Moselle Triangle as Patton's Third Army drove into Germany. The Germans thought we were going to head due east after crossing the Moselle River, and they had massed their tanks and infantry in front of us to stop our advance. But General Patton had the troops turn left and proceed north, parallel to the river. My unit was with them as they advanced through such German towns as Mürich, Saarburg, Ayl, Shoden, and Irsch.

A 3rd Army 155mm gun crew get ready to fire another round as smoke rises in background from shell-hit. This artillery could be four or five miles behind the line; it would require spotters to find the targets. Near Saarburg, Germany. U.S. Army Signal Corps; photograph by C.E. Sumners. Stamped: "Confidential. Passed for Publication as Censored. 24 FEB 1945."

Esch

We had just crossed the Moselle River at Esch and were under heavy fire from tanks. The Germans were amassing their troops in front of us. A tank at the head of our convoy hit a tank trap and everything stopped.

I pulled out of the convoy, parked the jeep behind a house and walked around to the doorway. A jeep stopped right in front where I

German prisoners, taken by 10th Armored Division of 3rd U.S. Army in Irsch, are marched toward tank block at end of street. Dead German soldiers and a live chicken on right side of street. U.S. Army Signal Corps; photograph by C.E. Sumners. Stamped: "Passed for Publication. Field Press Censor. 28 FEB 1945."

was standing, and I thought the person inside looked very familiar. So, I walked out to the jeep and discovered that the guy was Mike Hassett, a boy from my hometown. His father was a farmer as was my father; Mike and I had played on the same football team in high school.

He and I talked for a few minutes before the convoy began to roll once more, and I did not see Mike again until after the war. We now live a few miles from each other, and occasionally we get together to talk about the war.

The Pot Holder

Our group was well ahead of any mess hall setup, and we killed a calf that weighed about 400 pounds. My daddy was a butcher as well as a farmer, and I knew how to skin out a calf — you hang them with a stick, just like you would do with a hog. Some of the tankers helped me hang him up and skin him out. We gutted it down and took an old axe to chop up the meat. Later, I cooked steak for my unit, the tanker group that had helped me with the slaughter of the calf and for Lieutenant English of a photo unit that was attached to the Tenth Armored Division.

Tanks and 2½-ton GMC trucks of 10th Armored Division, 3rd U.S. Army, partly surround group of German prisoners rounded up by infantrymen of the Division in the vicinity of Trier, Germany. U.S. Army Signal Corps; photograph by C.E. Sumners. Stamped: "Passed for Publication. Field Press Censor. 9 MAR, 1945." Marked for radio transmission back to States.

Artillerymen of the 10th Armored Division, 3rd U.S. Army, inspect a captured German 88MM gun, taken intact in the garrison at Trier, Germany. Note dead Nazi in foreground. Jeep has 50 caliber machine gun attached. Shell casings from 88MM gun litter cobblestone street. U.S. Army Signal Corps; photograph by C.E. Sumners. Stamped: "Confidential. Not to Be Published. Field Press Censor. 9 MAR 1945."

We had a big barrel of wine in the cellar, some German Schnapps and plenty of black German bread. Someone had found a pound of butter and had put it down on a chair and one of the tankers sat down on it. We were looking for the butter and someone said, "Hey, there it is on the bottom of his pants!" Some of them were so drunk by this time that they were over there with knives scrapping this butter off the seat of his old canvas britches to put on their bread. This black German bread was really good, especially with orange marmalade spread on it.

Some two hours later, Lieutenant Moore and Lieutenant English, who had been off drinking away from the enlisted men, came back and they were both "polluted." Lieutenant Moore told me to go in there and fix him a steak sandwich, so I went into the kitchen. There was only one steak left, and I wanted it for myself, since I had fried steaks nearly all night while the others were eating it all up.

I found an old greasy black potholder and cut it up just where it would fit that black bread. I put it between two pieces and added plenty of catsup on top of the potholder. When I carried it back in there, the two lieutenants almost had a wrestling match to see who would get the steak sandwich. Lieutenant Moore won out — he grabbed it and bit into it. The bread slipped off the potholder, and the potholder flopped down while catsup ran down his chin.

Lieutenant English got on the floor and rolled. Moore was standing there with that bread in his hand and that old potholder hanging down over his chin. Every time Lieutenant English would see me from then on he would crack up laughing and say, "That had to be the funniest expression on any man's face that I had ever seen."

Tank of the 10th Armored Division, 3rd U.S. Army, moved into the town of Wittlich, Germany, through street lined with shell wrecked buildings. U.S. Army Signal Corps; photograph by C.E. Sumners. Stamped: "Passed for Publication 12 MAR 1945."

Third U.S. Army infantrymen advance up debris littered street in Wittlich, Germany. Just across the river, close to Esch. U.S. Army Signal Corps; photograph by C.E. Sumners. Stamped: "Passed for Publication. 12 MAR 1945. RADIO."

My Pistol and the Sniper

We were with the Tenth Armored Division somewhere in Germany, and there was a sniper across the road who had been firing at us. Our guys had been firing back, but the firing had stopped for a few minutes.

I had just gotten my gun back from ordnance. The barrel had corroded badly, and I was chewed out pretty good for letting it get in this condition. Well, I decided that I would test my gun to see if it would still fire after those ordnance folks had had it. So, I started shooting a couple of rounds toward the house where the sniper was located.

Colonel Cherry, who was in charge of this outfit, came storming up the ditch toward me hollering, "Who in the hell is doing that shooting?"

I said, "I was, Sir."

He said, "Let me tell you something, soldier. I have men going around behind that building to come up on the other side, and I had stopped all my men from firing. Now, if you fire one more round at that building over there, I am going to stop all my men from what they are doing, and I am going to send *you* down there to flush out that sniper!"

I said, "Yes, Sir. I read you loud and clear."

Trier

By March 2, 1945, the 10th Armored Division had taken the towns of Wittlich and Trier.

19

REFUGEES

In every war, the people that stand to lose the most have nothing to gain from the outcome of the conflict. I remember the scenes along the coast of France where the invasion took place. The Allies would take a town, then the Germans would counterattack and retake the town, and we would then recapture the town. By that time, the town would be totally destroyed from all the fighting to control the area. Many buildings would be completely demolished or badly damaged, and many of the businesses destroyed.

Knocked out American tank and dead Germans shown on narrow street between farm buildings which was tank block in Irsch, Germany, on the 3rd U.S. Army front. U.S. Army Signal Corps; photograph by C.E. Sumners. Stamped: "Passed for Publication. Field Press Censor. 28 FEB 1945." Marked for radio transmission back to States.

Most of the farms in France consisted of 30 acres or less and were a beautiful sight to see before they were pillaged or totally destroyed during various battles. After the war, many of the farms had mines in the fields, making it dangerous to farm because a land mine could blow up the horse, the tractor or even the French farmer plowing the fields.

The same was true for farms, cities and towns in Belgium and Germany.

Scenes of refugees fleeing from these places or returning to their homes are pictures that never leave your mind. These people left,

Vehicles of 10th Armored Division, 3rd U.S. Army, pass through shelled town of St. Wendel, Germany, during Division's drive toward the Rhine River. U.S. Army Signal Corps; photograph by C.E. Sumners. Stamped: "Passed for Publication. Field Press Censor. 22 MAR 1945."

not certain of where they were going or if they would ever return. They realized that if their homes did exist when they returned, they would most likely be pillaged or damaged beyond repair. What goods they carried with them might possibly be confiscated.

Many times the German soldiers would try to escape by hiding among evacuating civilians as they headed back from the front. They would also march the civilians out in front of their army to meet the Americans as they advanced, figuring that we would not shell or fire on the civilians while they (the soldiers) slipped out the back way.

After the war we would see caravans of refugees headed back to their particular towns and countries. Most of these refugees were going to Poland, and you could see them for miles and miles and miles covering the roads headed home. They were on bicycles, some walking, some pulling carts and some even in wheelbarrows. We saw some with a mule or cow hooked to and pulling a wagon with anything they had to take back with them.

They would eat anything they could find. Some were seen to boil grass that they found along the road. I saw them picking apples in a small apple orchard where the apples were small and still green, but it did not matter to them. When they left the orchard, all the apples were gone — eaten from the trees.

The main thing that I noticed about the caravans of refugees and slave laborers

Captured Germans. Hitler-Jugend on left. GI shows compassion by rolling a civilian in a wheel barrow. U.S. Army Signal Corps; photograph by C.E. Sumners. Stamped: "Confidential, Until Reclassified by Censor."

Refugees such as these would be sent out in front of German tanks and troops so U.S. forces would not fire on them. U.S. Army Signal Corps; photograph by C.E. Sumners. Stamped: "Confidential, Until Reclassified by Censor."

Captured military installation in Germany. General view of huge transit area located near Trier, Germany, where former prisoners of the Germans were cared for by military government teams. Liberated people were cared for here before being returned to their homelands. U.S. Army Signal Corps; photograph by C.E. Sumners. Stamped: "Passed for Publication. Field Press Censor. 22 MAR 1945."

Russian mother with her baby walks past an American halftrack parked in the yard of the displacement camp near Trier. U.S. Army Signal Corps; photograph by C.E. Sumners. Stamped: "Passed for Publication. Field Press Censor. 22 MAR 1945."

Russian family recently liberated by U.S. troops gather round a fire cooking their evening meal in the displacement camp. U.S. Army Signal Corps; photograph by C.E. Sumners. Stamped: "Passed for Publication. Field Press Censor. 22 MAR 1945."

Recently liberated Russians singing and making merry at the displacement camp. U.S. Army Signal Corps; photograph by C.E. Sumners. Stamped: "Passed for Publication Field Press Censor 22 MAR 1945."

Engineers repairing bridge somewhere in France. Note the destroyed home in the background. U.S. Army Signal Corps; photograph by C.E. Sumners. Marked: "Confidential, Until Reclassified by Censor."

going home was the fact that there were practically no young people in the groups and certainly no small children. Most of the people looked much older than their age. They had been worked so hard and starved to skin and bones in those camps, but ...

They were heading home — to reclaim properties that possibly no longer existed and to find members of their families most of whom were, in reality, already dead.

20

HITLER YOUTH

We arrived at a small village near Trier late one afternoon and moved into an un-occupied house where the people had left to get out of the battle area and retreated with the German army. When we moved into a house, we would usually try to take care of it, if there were no display of Nazi type material around. But if the house had a picture of Hitler or other Nazi stuff, we would not be too particular with what we did to it.

There was a German family that lived next door, and they had a boy about 12 years old. Every time we would get back to the house where we were staying, this boy would never speak; he would just stand outside and glare hatefully at us. I had walked around behind the house one day, and I saw him sneaking out toward an old shed out back.

He came out of the shed with a rifle, so I slipped around and came out in the alley behind him, walking up on him just as he leveled the old rifle over a well curbing. I guessed that he had intended to shoot at some of the soldiers across the street where an outfit had just moved in the day before.

I pulled my pistol and told him that if he did not put the rifle down, I was going to shoot him. He didn't appear to be scared, but he looked at me and finally put the old rifle down on the well curbing.

I put my pistol back in the holster, picked up the rifle, ejected all the shells from it and slammed the bolt home. I was not aware that one shell had stuck in the old barrel, however. Intending to break the rifle, I hit the barrel against the well curbing. Suddenly I felt a hot streak across my upper thigh with a lot of powder smoke coming out of the barrel of the gun. This smoke got in my eyes and scared me nearly to death. I thought, "Goodness sakes, I have gone and shot myself!"

I turned around, and this little German kid was laughing at me. I was scared, em-barrassed and angry — all at the same time. I pulled my pistol and put it under his nose, and for just a few seconds I came close to killing him. I had the urge to shoot him so badly that I could taste it!

A lieutenant and a couple of guys that were across the street came running over to us to see what was going on. I told the officer that this kid was taking a bead on them with his rifle and that, while I was stopping him from firing, the gun went off. The lieutenant said they would take care of the kid and grabbed him by the nape of the neck. They took him across the street, put him in a jeep and, I suppose, took him to a POW cage.

That young boy was probably a Hitler-Jugend, one of the kids that Hitler had said were his youth men of future Germany. Their mothers had to prove that they were of pure German descent, and the fathers were "select" German soldiers specifically chosen to breed these "superpeople."

These youngsters were cared for by the government. They were schooled from birth in military tactics and things pertaining to war. In this program, they studied mathematics, engineering and languages that would be helpful to them for future war leadership.

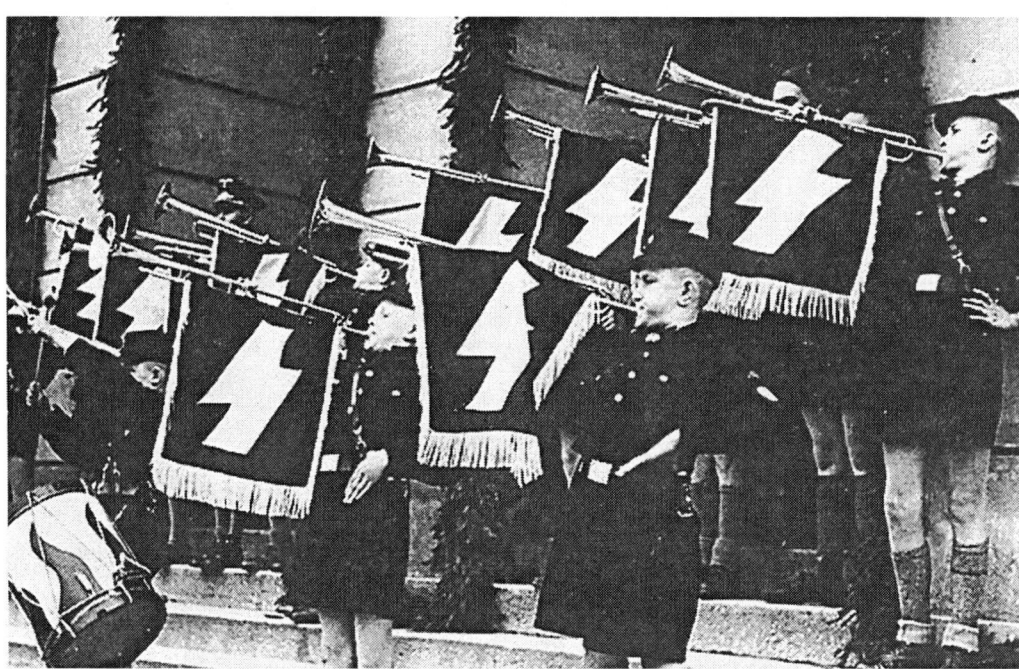

Hitler Youth perform in the Hour of Commemoration in front of the town hall in Tomaszow, Poland, in 1941. Their flags bear the ancient Germanic Sig-Rune "S" symbolic of victory. National Archives, College Park, MD.

Ninety percent of those kids spoke very good English. One of them told me that they planned to conquer the world and that the French, English and all other European countries would come under their rule. He was certain they would need to speak many languages when they ruled the world.

The leaders of this youth movement had much more control over the children's lives than their own parents did. Many of these kids had been taken away from their mothers and fathers, who were secondary figures to them. These youths were rewarded for certain phases of training, and they received medals, ribbons and engraved knives for things they would do for their leaders.

Tankmen of 10th Armored Division, 3rd U.S. Army, flush enemy sniper out of railroad culvert near Frankenstein, Germany. U.S. Army Signal Corps; photograph by C.E. Sumners. Stamped: "Passed for Publication. Field Press Censor. 24 MAR 1945."

Left: Dead Nazi bazookaman huddled in a foxhole after being killed by infantrymen of 6th Armored Division of General Patton's 3rd Army near Windischleuba, Germany. (Notice the bullethole in helmet.) U.S. Army Signal Corps; photograph by C.E. Sumners. Stamped: "Passed for Publication. Field Press Censor. 18 APR 1945."

We ran into quite a few of these Hitler-Jugends right before the war ended. We were with the Tenth Armored Division and were approaching an intersection in some small town when some of these kids knocked out a tank up ahead. Our tanks and infantrymen opened fire on the house they were in and blew it apart. Several German soldiers came out of the house and started across an open field. Our people opened up on them with 50 caliber machine guns and shot them down.

I went out in the field with a couple of infantrymen to get a picture of the tanks and infantry passing across that intersection. We saw one of the German soldiers trying to crawl around, moaning and groaning. When we went over to this person, we discovered a girl about 14 years old and she had been shot through the leg. Medics came to bandage her and took her off to what I am sure was a POW cage.

Several of these young Germans had been killed. After looking at them, I figured that the oldest one could not have been over 15 years old. They were usually mixed in with old men. Some of their uniforms were not even regular issue, but rather looked more like some of our Boy Scout uniforms.

21

Patton at the Rhine

After Trier, we began steady advances with the Tenth Armored through conflicts in Wedern, Waldholzbach, Gronig, St. Wendel, Frankenstein, Neustadt and Malsfeld in the push to the Rhine River and beyond.

One day in late March while we were preparing to cross the Rhine, I was at headquarters waiting for Lieutenant Threlkel to cut some orders for our unit. He came in and said that the general needed a photographer right away. He asked me to drive Grant, a still photographer, on this assignment, so I said, "O.K., I don't have anything else to do." Grant gave me his little 35mm Leica camera to hang around my neck, and he got his Speed Graphic 4×5.

We went out to the jeep and fell in behind General Patton and another jeep carrying two officers. We headed out and drove about 15 or 20 miles before turning off onto a dirt road. We saw several tanks along the way, and General Patton would have his driver slow down or stop so he could stand up in his jeep to wave and yell at his troops—to let them know who he was and that the general was coming through. His jeep was special with armor plating on the sides, and all the troops knew him and his jeep, because he did these things quite often.

He had his driver pull up to the banks of the Rhine River. I still had not been told what we were there for. We got out of our jeep and walked up to where the general was, and he immediately asked Grant, "Are you ready, boy? I'm not going to hold this much longer."

And he unbuttons his pants and starts to urinate in the Rhine River. Of course, I shot a couple of pictures with my little old Leica while Grant shot a couple or three with his larger Speed Graphic using a film pack.

General Patton said, "I might just send one of these pictures to Hitler." He then proceeded to get back into his jeep.

We went back to headquarters and were sitting there in the photo section when

Colonel Hammond, one of the officers with General Patton when we took the pictures, came in. He asked who was the cameraman that took those pictures of the general at the river. Grant immediately said that he was the one that took the pictures. Col. Hammond told Grant to give him the film because "the general has changed his mind. He doesn't want that printed or published."

Grant gave him the film pack. I was still speechless anyway and did not think about the film in my small camera, and Grant didn't think to tell them about my taking those pictures either.

Well, one day about ten years ago, a man that worked with me at Mueller Company said that he had heard that I had been a photographer with General Patton in World War II. I answered that yes, I had been. He said, "My brother was also with Patton in Europe, and he has a picture of General Patton pissing in the Rhine River."

It hit me like a ton of bricks! That had to be the picture I had taken with Grant's little 35mm Leica camera. How this ever got printed, I have no idea. As far as I know one of the officers with Patton could have had a camera, but I don't believe they did. Grant had been dead for many years, so there was no way I could check that out.

The man swears that his brother had this picture. I tried to get him to get the picture and offered to pay him any amount to get it. He tried, but his brother was in a nursing home and out of his head, and this guy didn't get along with his sister-in-law too well. So, he never got the picture, but I'm sure that was the print of the picture I took of Patton pissing in the Rhine.

I would like to have had this photograph just to prove my story. Grant is dead, and I'm sure most of the others are dead also, but such a long time has passed and the picture was lost or destroyed by relatives of this man.

Cooler heads on his staff convinced him that it was not a wise move, but General Patton had enough brass that he, I'm sure, would have actually sent this picture to Hitler.

I have recently seen a picture on an Internet website with a caption that indicates Patton is urinating in the Rhine. That is not the scene we photographed — the General was standing on the riverbank, not some pontoon boats, and everyone was watching him.

22

TANKS

When you think of the Third Army, you automatically think of General George Patton. And when you think of General Patton, you think of tanks, because tanks were what he was skilled in. He was probably as good a tank commander as anyone, maybe with the exception of the German general, Rommel.

General Patton believed in moving fast as lightning, and the tank was a way to cover a lot of ground in a short period of time. Many of the footsloggers—the infantrymen—would be a little envious of the guys going by in a tank until they saw a tank that had been hit by a shell or with a bazooka.

A tanker's life was rough. If he were in the lead tank, he would probably have had three or four knocked out from under him. If he were still able to fight, he would get in another one and go back to battle again—time after time. In contrast, the air force guys flew 30 missions and were able to rotate home. A tank driver would ask, "How many tanks do I have to have destroyed from under me before they say 'you've had enough, so you get to rotate home'?"

We had several different size tanks. Right at the end of the war, we had the M32, which was a 35-ton tank that had a 90mm gun on it and was quite effective in battle. We also had the M18 that was only 19 tons, but it would go 60 miles an hour

Tank crewmen work to dig out their tank that is stuck in the mud. U.S. Army Signal Corps; photograph by C.E. Sumners. Stamped: "Confidential, Until Reclassified by Censor."

Awaiting Kyll crossing at Auw, Germany, are 3rd U.S. Army tankmen PFC Henry Brooker, La Grange, GA, PFC Van Gorp, Sioux Center Falls, IA, Pvt. Masbroker, Hoboken, NJ, and Sgt. Ernest Grindeland, Thief River Falls, MN ... and five white rabbits! U.S. Army Signal Corps; photograph by C.E. Sumners. Stamped: "Confidential. Not to Be Published. Field Press Censor. 10 MAR 1945."

or better. It only had about ¾-inch armor plating around its body, so about any type of shell would penetrate it and knock it out of action.

The M18 was a "hit and run" type of tank; it would fire, maneuver, and then run like blazes to get away from the fire power of the superior German tanks. It had an air-cooled engine and was very fast. It could be used in the desert in a hot climate or in the snow of a Belgian winter. It had a big engine, and every morning the tanker would have to hand crank it about 35 times to get everything working properly before actually starting the engine with the automatic starter.

The largest tank in World War II was the German Elephant tank. I made pictures of this tank showing how two tanks protected each other. On other tanks the guns would move a full 360°, but the guns on this Elephant tank would only swing about 180°. The Germans would use these tanks in pairs—sitting back to back to protect each other's rear.

This tank had thick armor plating along the sides, and it was almost impossible for a shell to knock it out of action by hitting it on the sides. A lieutenant came up with a very ingenious idea that you could knock out the German tank if you fired the shells and ricocheted them off the pavement into the underbelly, which only had about one inch of armor plating. The two tanks that I filmed had been knocked out of action using this method.

A knocked out German Elephant tank — weighing 100 tons and carrying a 120mm gun — receives an inspection from G.I.s of the 10th Armored Division, 3rd U.S. Army, who were responsible for its capture near Neustadt, Germany. U.S. Army Signal Corps; photograph by C.E. Sumners. Stamped: "Confidential. Not to be Published. Field Press Censor. 26 MAR 1945."

Two German Elephant tanks that were knocked out by 10th Armored Division, 3rd U.S. Army troops, at the outskirts of Neustadt, Germany. These were the largest tanks of World War II. They usually sat back to back in a maneuver to protect each other, because their guns could only turn 180°. U.S. Army Signal Corps; photograph by C.E. Sumners. Stamped: "Confidential. Not to be Published. Field Press Censor. 26 MAR 1945."

Interior view of German Elephant tank, weighing 100 tons and carrying a 120mm gun. L-R: unfired shells in their cartons, gunner's seat, and recoil mechanism. Due to heavy frontal armor, this tank is almost impossible to knock out from the front. However, the rear is very vulnerable. This tank was knocked out near Neustadt, Germany, by the 10th Armored Division, 3rd U.S. Army. U.S. Army Signal Corps; photograph by C.E. Sumners. Stamped: "Confidential. Not for Publication. Field Press Censor. 26 MAR 1945."

Damage to a German Elephant tank. Photo shows hits scored. U.S. Army Signal Corps; photograph by C.E. Sumners. Stamped: "Confidential. Not to Be Published. Field Press Censor. 26 MAR 1945."

6th Armored Division tanks and half-tracks, with the 3rd U.S. Army, fan out in an open field near Lucka, Germany, awaiting order to attack. U.S. Army Signal Corps; photograph by C.E. Sumners. Stamped: "Passed for Publication. Field Press Censor. 18 APR 1945."

Many times you could hear a tank battle, but unless you were on high ground, you would not be able to see the enemy tanks. Only on rare occasions would you see tanks directly firing at one another. We did see one such battle with an American tank and a German tank. The German tank was finally able to knock out the American tank, but I was too far away to get a combat picture of this action. It would have just looked like a speck on the print.

Usually, the tankers would go out in a group of four tanks, and one of these would be pulling the ammunition trailer. They all had a certain position in the tank formation. The tankers were trained and drilled over and over, but in real action all this was sometimes not followed, as terrain, location and the enemy would determine what they did and how they did it.

The difference between someone who is trained well and someone who's not is very evident in war. You might sometimes wonder why are we doing this same thing over and over in training, but once you get into combat, you can get so scared you do not know what you are doing, or you don't even know your name. Then you realize that, because of this monotonous drilling, you can still perform the job you have been trained to do. Then you appreciate those weeks of training that you hated, and you are able to function just like a robot and do things without thinking.

Tank destroyer lays down flat trajectory fire on the smoking town of Koltzschen, near Rochlitz, Germany, as 6th Armored Division of Gen. Patton's 3rd Army sweeps through area. U.S. Army Signal Corps; photograph by C.E. Sumners. Stamped: "Passed for Publication. Field Press Censor. 18 APR 1945."

My brother Paul was a tank driver in World War II. On March 30, 1945, they were engaged in a tank battle with the Germans near the town of Zweickel, Germany. Caught in a crossfire, Paul's M-18 tank was firing to the right and they were hit from a crossfire from the left.

There were four tanks in the third platoon. Paul's tank was the fourth tank in the convoy and the third tank to be hit. The Germans let the first tank go on by. They then hit the second tank between the turret and the tracks, so it could not move on. Then they hit the third tank, which was the one where the smoke pots and ammunition were stored. That tank was disabled and three people in it were wounded.

Paul Sumners remembers:

> The Germans hit my tank from the left side with a 75mm round that came through the instrument panel of my M18 tank and across my body. Since I was driving with a periscope, I was sitting much lower than usual (you are sitting almost on the ground when you drive by periscope). The round hit our tank's transmission, cut off the head of the assistant driver and wounded the assistant gunner and myself. I had two shrapnel shards in my neck, two in my side and two in my shoulder, all of which had to be removed later.

Crew of a 3rd U.S. Army Tank Destroyer Unit rest alongside a new type M-18 Tank Destroyer, outside the burning town of Shoden, Germany, then being assaulted by 3rd U.S. Army troops. This was the type of tank driven by Charles Sumners' brother, Paul. It carried a crew of five: driver, asst. driver, sergeant, gunner, asst. gunner. It was a 19-ton tank destroyer, with 76mm gun and a 50 caliber mounted on right, that could travel at 62 mph. U.S. Army Signal Corps; photograph by C.E. Sumners. Stamped: "Confidential. Passed for Publication as Censored. Field Press Censor 27 FEB 1945."

We got out of the tank and the Germans opened up on us with machine guns as we ran about 100 yards toward a ditch for cover. One of the tracer bullets hit the strap on the side of my helmet and made a ping sound as it went by.

We lay in the water-filled ditch for about one and a half hours until it got dark. Then Sergeant Hennings and I walked about a mile or so back to Zweickel and got a jeep driver to take us back to get the other two wounded men.

They took us to a field hospital, and I stayed there for two weeks. The hospital had 200 beds and all of those beds were filled with wounded GIs. After two weeks, I told the nurse I was leaving, and she said, "You can't go."

I told her, "You either give me my uniform or I will leave this hospital with this split-tail gown on." Well, they finally let me leave, and I rode 185 miles back to my outfit in an ambulance.

You don't realize what it is when you get hit the first time, but then when you go back into action after that, you know what could happen to you. That going back was possibly the second scariest time I had had — the most scared was when we were hit. So going back into another tank and knowing what could happen was a "gut-wrenching" event.

Sgt. Paul Sumners, brother of Charles Sumners, drove an M-18 tank destroyer. 809th Tank Destroyer, Gen. Patton's 3rd U.S. Army, Ardennes and Germany, 1945.

When we were hit, the inside of the tank looked like a huge sparkler from the metal hitting other metals. Had I been driving in the normal position when we were hit, it would have cut me in two. If it had been a high explosive instead of armor piercing, there would have been no way that any of us in the front of the tank could have lived.

It's amazing what people can do when they are scared. One of the guys injured when our tank was hit ran on an ankle that we later discovered was only held on by the skin, and he could not even stand on it later.

Our tank was an M18 with a 76mm gun attached to it. I had not lain down to sleep for eight days and nights before we were hit. We had been on the run and in action. I would grab five, ten minutes or sometimes an hour of sleep sitting on the seat of that tank.

Our 166th photo unit was with a tank group in a small town in Germany. There were two tanks about 100 yards off to our right in an open field and two more were on our left flank. There were other tanks plus half-tracks in front of us and armored infantrymen all around. We could hear the tanks that were ahead firing, and there was return fire by the German tanks.

Suddenly I saw the infantrymen dismount the half-tracks, seeking shelter and looking toward the building on the side of the street. I decided this was no safe place for someone in a jeep, so I turned my jeep left on a side road. I was hoping that I could circle around, get back on the road we came in on and head back out of town. I certainly did not want to get caught in the middle of a tank battle.

I headed down this street, but it did not circle back to the left as I had figured it would; instead, it circled back to the right. As I rounded the corner, we ran right upon a German tank some 30 yards ahead with its gun pointed straight at the jeep. I slammed on the brakes and jumped out of the jeep, preparing to make a run for it, but the other guys just sat in the jeep — dumb-founded.

Suddenly, the turret on the tank opened up, and I saw an arm stick up waving a white flag, handkerchief or some white cloth. This, of course, was the sign of surrender. The flag-waver helped a wounded buddy out of the tank, and they both climbed down to the ground with their hands up in the air. As we took them prisoner, I noticed that their tank was smoking. It had apparently taken a direct hit and was put out of action.

We took the prisoners down the street and turned them over to the armored infantrymen. I wheeled that jeep around, headed back to the location of the half-tracks and turned right onto the escape route out of town. We had gone about a half-mile before I slowed down, and Meyer said, "Well, I'll be damned."

I said, "What is your problem? We got out of there all right, and you didn't get hurt did you?"

He said, "No, I didn't get hurt, but that was probably as good as any combat pictures you could ever hope to take. And here are four men with cameras, who are combat cameramen, and we sat there with a smoking German tank and two Germans crawling out waving a white flag — and *none* of us made a picture of what was going on!"

I said, "Well, at that point, I was not too concerned about taking pictures of combat or pictures of anything — period! All I was concerned about was getting out of that situation alive. If that tank had not been knocked out by our tanks, it would have blown us to kingdom come."

So, you never really know what is going to happen in war or how you are going to react to a situation. Later, when I had time to really think about what had just happened, I thought about what a missed opportunity it had been to take a great combat picture. However, I also realized that we were all lucky that the tank was not still in action and that we were still alive after this adventure.

I had become acquainted with many officers in tank outfits, but one that I was especially close to was a major that drove a small M-8 tank with rubber tires that carried

German prisoners used as work crew. Tanks of 6th Armored Division, 3rd Army, cross bridge over Mulde River at Rochlitz, Germany, after prisoners, left, had cleared road block. U.S. Army Signal Corps; photograph by C.E. Sumners. Stamped: "Confidential. Not to Be Published. Field Press Censor. 18 APR 1945."

only a 20mm gun on it. It was a fast tank, but the armor plating was so thin, you could shoot through the side of it with an M-1 rifle or maybe even a carbine.

Charles Wright was a very young fellow to be a major, but he was a fine man. I had always thought the major ranking was a wasted rank — not high enough to be over a battalion and too much rank to be over a company. Usually, the majors were just executive officers or those that ran errands for a general in the division.

This particular major and I got to know each other at a river crossing where the river was being covered with smoke. We were together for several days while this was happening, and later on I bumped into him again.

Wright, Meyer and I were on a hill overlooking a small town near the Saar River when a German officer came out of the town with a white flag on a stick and wanted to know if we would take him and his men prisoners. The air force had bombed and strafed the town, plus artillery and tanks had shelled it. There were about 200 Germans still left alive in the town and they were shot up pretty badly.

The major told them that yes, we would take them prisoners. He and Meyer left me guarding the 200 prisoners while they went down into the town to gather up cameras and any other type of items that they might find that we could use. They came back with a big basket full of cameras, binoculars, Luger pistols and fairy guns that they had found.

We put these items in this little M-8 tank that the major was driving, planning to divide up these items later on. Well, later never came. Sometime the next morning, he

German prisoners near Ayl, Germany. U.S. Army Signal Corps; photograph by C.E. Sumners. Stamped: "Confidential, Until Reclassified by Censor."

Maj. Charles Wright, left, Sterling, IL, a 3rd U.S. Army Engineer officer, emerges from smoke covered area near Ayl, Germany. Smoke pots along road offered cover for 3rd Army troops pushing across the Saar River. U.S. Army Signal Corps; photograph by C.E. Sumners. Stamped: "Passed for Publication as Censored. Field Press Censor. 25 FEB 1945 RADIO."

got into a battle with a German SS troop, and one of them fired a bazooka into his tank. The tank was destroyed, all our loot was burned up, and our major friend was killed. He was such a fine man, and we hated to lose him.

Usually you try not to become too close with other soldiers in combat, because their loss would affect you so much. You see them one day; then maybe the next day, they have "bought the farm." That was the way the war went.

23

ENGINEERS

I know the infantrymen and tankers got a lot of credit and it was well deserved, but the engineers were the unsung heroes of World War II as far as I am concerned. Many times they had to go in first to remove obstacles (like blowing up pillboxes) so that the infantry or tankers could have a path to reach their objectives. Many times they were the last to leave, for when GIs left, the engineers had to stay behind to blow up bridges, plant mines and other such chores to impede the enemy advancement.

One time we were right outside a small town that had been shelled so much that only hulls of buildings were still standing. The engineers prepared to lay a bunch of mines across the road right outside this town to keep the enemy from sneaking in during the night. They already had the mines activated and loaded in the back of a 2½-ton truck, and they hit a bump in the road.

Soldier looks at damage done to a bridge by bombs or mortar. U.S. Army Signal Corps; photograph by C.E. Sumners. Stamped: "Confidential, Until Reclassified by Censor."

The mines evidently bounced up in the back of the truck and detonated on impact when they came back down. The only thing left of that truck and the two engineers in it was the front bumper. The brick and masonry buildings were blown away, and the truck was in thousands of pieces. Many times something like that happened. One charge would ignite the other and there would be a chain reaction. I have thought about this incident often, and I am still chilled by the fact that a bump in a road caused these two GIs to lose their lives in such a manner.

Land Mines

We were at Nehou right after we first landed in Normandy, and we went back to the beaches to photograph an engineer company that was taking up mines out of fields and roads.

Many times, in an open field, the mines were set in a pattern, and once the pattern was figured out the mines were fairly easy to find. We watched with keen interest as one pair of guys worked this particular area.

One guy would go ahead with his metal detector, and locate and mark the mine. Then this redheaded sergeant would carefully dig out around the mine and check it out. He would then disarm the detonator and remove it. In the bottom of the detonator was a little hole, in which he would insert a pin or a nail. Then he could unscrew the detonator and take it out. Now the detonator had a charge in it that sounded like a 22-caliber rifle when it went off. This is what causes the mine to explode.

Well, it was a hot day and the sergeant that was disarming the mines was sweating from the hot weather and the nerves that come from this dangerous job.

Engineers searching for and disarming land mines. U.S. Army Signal Corps; photograph by C.E. Sumners. Stamped: "Confidential, Until Reclassified by Censor."

A quartermaster lieutenant and his driver came up in their jeep from the beach where they were unloading the ships. This officer began to ask lots of questions, and I could tell that the sergeant was getting very irritated. He didn't want to be distracted from the dangerous job he was doing. Just the least little mistake, and he would have been blown to bits.

He finally got the dirt from around this one mine and finished dismantling it. Then he turned around, walked up to the lieutenant and handed him the detonator. The lieutenant accidentally pressed the three prongs that stick up there on the detonator, and it, of course, fired off like a rifle shot. That lieutenant jumped about ten feet high in the air, whirled around, jumped in his jeep, and they headed back to the beach.

Sometime they would mine an area in a random, no pattern, way. We were going down a road when we saw an old German civilian who had stepped on a land mine that had blown his foot off. He was lying in a field with his leg sticking up in the air.

One of our captains with the medical corps went out into this mined field, bandaged the old man's leg, then turned around and walked back to his jeep. He sent two soldiers with a litter carriage to get the man out to the edge of the road so they could carry him back to a hospital.

It took a lot of nerve for these soldiers to go through that mined field to get to this old German. I just watched with all due respect as this took place.

We were with the engineers while they were trying to put a pontoon bridge across the Moselle River. The sun was shining, and it was a quiet time. The Germans, it turned out, were sitting and waiting on the high ground on the other side of the river.

Of course, the first thing I always did when we went into a combat zone would be to turn my jeep around and park headed out toward the rear to safety. This saved a lot of time in case of enemy fire.

Lieutenant Moore, Russ Meyer, Joe Lapine and I got out of the jeep and headed down toward the river. The engineers had about one fourth of the pontoon boats out. We had not gotten but about 15 or 20 yards when the Germans opened up firing on us, and they blew the bridge out of the water.

We dived into a ditch close to a bunch of the old pontoon boats that had not been used yet and were turned upside down. As soon as possible, we made a dash back to our jeep, but Lapine was so scared that he left his camera in the ditch.

I told him to go back and get it, and he did. When he got back, he jumped over the spare tire into the jeep, and we headed out of there.

The engineers lost a lot of people that morning. They finally had to abandon their plans to cross the river at that location. Later we went down below that area and were able to cross on a bridge that had been built by some other engineering group.

There were many tragic and scary things that happened during the war, but there were also lots of amusing incidents. Many times after you had been in combat and managed to get back to a safe zone, everything would seem to be really funny.

Lieutenant Moore and I went down to film our troops trying to cross the Saar River, and a chemical warfare outfit was there to make a smoke screen for the river crossing. These generators had to be hand-cranked, and the engineers had to continuously add materials to the generators to get the smoke to come out.

The Germans could not see us because of the smoke, so they were not firing on us. The infantry had dug a lot of foxholes along the bank of the river, and we headed toward them hoping to get close enough to take some pictures of our boys crossing the river. I had the still camera and Moore had the movie camera.

Vehicles crossing bridge recently constructed by engineers. Somewhere in Germany, 1945. U.S. Army Signal Corps; photograph by C.E. Sumners. Stamped: "Confidential, Until Reclassified by Censor."

Bridge built by U.S. Army Corps of Engineers over a destroyed bridge. U.S. Army Signal Corps; photograph C.E. Sumners. Stamped: "Confidential, Until Reclassified by Censor."

Soldiers of the 161st Chemical Smoke Generating Company, U.S. 3rd Army, move a barrel of oil in preparation for refilling an M-2 smoke generator, which spews forth a heavy cloud of white smoke. These men are engaged in laying a smoke screen to cover bridge building activities across the Saar River near Wallerfangen, Germany. National Archives, College Park, MD; photograph by Rothenberger, Dec. 11, 1944.

Engineers of 10th Armored Division, 3rd Army, use bulldozer to fill in shell crater in road near Frankenstein, Germany. They are repairing road for passage of armor and troops of 10th Armored Division and 80th Infantry Regiment, 3rd U.S. Army. U.S. Army Signal Corps; photograph by C.E. Sumners. Stamped: "Passed for Publication. Field Press Censor. 24 MAR 1945."

Just as we got down to the river, the wind changed and blew all the smoke away from us, and we were left wide open with no smoke protection. There were some oats growing about three or four inches high in this open field, and the Germans started to fire mortars at us. Some of them hit in the water, but some others hit near us and we headed for those foxholes. I jumped into one and Moore jumped into another.

After a few minutes, I could hear the grinding noise of a movie camera, and I thought, "Surely, he's not up during this mortar barrage shooting picture!"

A few minutes later, the wind changed again and started blowing the smoke back toward the Germans as it was supposed to do. Feeling that it was safe to come out of the foxhole, I got out and asked Lieutenant Moore if he was filming during the mortar attack.

He said, "No, Charlie. I dived into the foxhole, and I was so scared that I had my finger on the camera trigger. It was a couple of minutes before I realized I was taking pictures of the interior of the foxhole."

24

CONFLICTS IN GERMANY

After Trier, we traveled with the 10th Armored Division as they began steady advances through the Saarland. We were in conflicts at places such as Wedern, Waldholzbach, Gronig, St. Wendel, Frankenstein (Darmstadt), Neustadt and Malsfeld in the push to the Rhine River and beyond.

Crop marks indicate that evaluator thinks photographer should have been at the marked spot to take the photograph. Infantrymen of the 10th Armored Division, 3rd U.S. Army, lie prone to escape the observation and fire of the enemy, hidden in the woods near Wedern, Germany. U.S. Army Signal Corps; photograph by C.E. Sumners. Stamped: "Confidential. Passed for Publication as Censored. 20 MAR 1945."

L-R: American tank, jeep, spotter and gunner on halftrack using a 50 caliber machine gun. Halftrack of 10th Armored Division, 3rd U.S. Army, fires into woods on hillside to halt escape of Germans from Gronig, Germany. U.S. Army Signal Corps; photograph by C.E. Sumners. Stamped: "Confidential. Passed for Publication as Censored. Field Press Censor. 21 MAR 1945."

Observation outpost. Smoke over the river in background. Infantrymen of the 10th Armored Division, 3rd U.S. Army, wait in their foxholes for orders to push forward, near Waldholzbach, Germany. U.S. Army Signal Corps; photograph by C.E. Sumners. Stamped: "Passed for Publication. Field Press Censor. 20 MAR 1945."

T/5 Charles Sumners examines the sieve-like remains of a German railroad freight car found in the railway yards at Neustadt, Germany, after recent capture of the town. U.S. Army Signal Corps; photograph by C.E. Sumners. Stamped: "Passed for Publication. 24 MAR 1945."

Vehicles of 10th Armored Division, 3rd U.S. Army, are parked in square of St. Wendel, Germany. White surrender flags hang from some windows in the town. U.S. Army Signal Corps; photograph by C.E. Sumners. Stamped: "Passed for Publication. Field Press Censor. 22 MAR 1945."

Infantrymen of 80th Division, 3rd U.S. Army, shown during advance through forest and mountains in Germany in German drive toward Rhine River. They are advancing in a combined action with the 10th Armored Division, 3rd U.S. Army. Note old abandoned wagon on side of the road. U.S. Army Signal Corps; photograph by C.E. Sumners. Stamped: "Passed for Publication. Field Press Censor. 24 MAR 1945."

25

GERMANY WITH THE SIXTH ARMORED DIVISION

By April 1945, we were well into Germany, traveling with the Sixth Armored Division of the Third Army.

Two towns stand out in particular. The first was Oberdorla, which, after the war and until the "Wall" came down, was located in the Eastern Zone. It was in Oberdorla that I took a picture that was selected by Army Pictorial Services as one of the 100 best photos of the European Theater. It and one other taken in the same town were among a collection selected by combat cameramen for the International Combat Camera Association's publication, *Combat Cameraman.*

Infantrymen of 6th Armored Division, 3rd U.S. Army, pass dead American killed by sniper in Oberdorla, Germany. This photo was chosen as one of the "Best 100 Photos of the European Theater." Credit U.S. Army Signal Corps; photog. CE Sumners.

I was attached to the infantry division as they were going street to street and door to door to flush out the German snipers. Some of these snipers were soldiers, but many of them were civilians. I had stopped to take out a film pack from my musette bag to reload my camera when an infantryman passed me. He had just gone about five or ten feet, right by an alley, when he was

Infantrymen of 6th Armored Division, 3rd U.S. Army, advancing cautiously through streets of Oberdorla, Germany. U.S. Army Signal Corps; photograph by C.E. Sumners. April 4, 1945.

shot and killed by one of the snipers. Had I not stopped to reload my camera, I would have possibly been the one killed.

I took a picture there, with this dead American soldier in the foreground. But sometimes, I wonder: was it blind luck or maybe the prayers of family and friends that kept me alive? Who knows?

The second town of particular interest was Mühlhausen.

When we left one place and went to another, we would go through G-2 or the intelligence section to look at a strategy map to find out exactly where all the units were and where the front line was located. The photographers were possibly the only enlisted, noncommissioned soldiers who were allowed to go into the intelligence section and get such information. We were allowed to do this because we had General Eisenhower passes that allowed us to go any place we needed to go in our jobs.

We looked at the strategy map and decided to go to Mühlhausen. This town was supposed to be free and cleared of German troops as one of our outfits had apparently already gone through the town.

We arrived at Mühlhausen just before it was getting dark, found a hotel that was a big three-story building, and moved right in. We didn't have to check into the hotel, because as "conquering heroes," we could just go in, pick out a room we liked and occupy it as long as we were in a town. We got some sleeping robes and went to bed.

The next morning, Lieutenant Moore came in, shook me awake, and told me to go

Photograph taken from 2nd story window of local hotel. Tanks, vehicles, and infantrymen of CCB, 6th Armored Division, 3rd U.S. Army, gather in a square of Mülhausen, Germany, the center of which is rapidly filling with German prisoners taken in the 3rd Army drive into Germany. U.S. Army Signal Corps; photograph by C.E. Sumners. Stamped: "Passed for Publication. Field Press Censor. 8 APR 1945."

German prisoners captured by the 6th Armored Division, 3rd U.S. Army, in Mülhausen, Germany, are lined up in the town square to be marched away to a prisoner of war enclosure in the rear of the lines. U.S. Army Signal Corps; photograph by C.E. Sumners. Stamped: "Passed for Publication. Field Press Censor. 8 APR 1945 RADIO."

look out of the window. Out in the square down below, were a bunch of GIs with about 300 German POWs who had surrendered to them early that morning. We found out that when our infantry arrived in town that morning, these Germans were waiting there with a white flag to surrender.

So, we had spent the night in this town with these Germans holding it, and we didn't even know it. We had had a good night's sleep, and it did not bother us after the fact. We had been lucky that, when we arrived in Mühlhausen, the German soldiers were occupied at the other end of town and did not observe us coming.

Other towns, some hard to find on a map, are vividly stamped in the memory bank — Waldkoffel, Meyhen, Theisen, Lucka, Windischleuba, Koltzschen (near Rochlitz), Rochlictz (near the Mulde River), and Waldkeppel. We went as far as Leipzig before meeting the Russians and returning to France.

6th Armored's infantry firing at enemy positions at Windischleuba, Germany, 1945. Photograph by C.E. Sumners.

6th Armored Division, 3rd U.S. Army Tank passes a burning German vehicle after a furious battle in the town of Theisen, Germany. U.S. Army Signal Corps; photograph by C.E. Sumners. Stamped: "Passed for Publication. Field Press Censor. 18 APR 1945."

Tank men of 6th Armored Division of Gen. Patton's 3rd Army rescue rabbits from burning hutch in newly captured Windischleuba. U.S. Army Signal Corps; photograph by C.E. Sumners. Stamped: "Passed for Publication. Field Press Censor. 18 APR 1945."

A piper cub taking off on a German air field just captured by CC B, 6th Armored Division, 3rd U.S. Army, near Mülhausen, Germany. U.S. Army Signal Corps; photograph by C.E. Sumners. Stamped: "Restricted. Not to Be Published. Field Press Censor. 10 APR 1945."

Captured German plane. An ME-110 in a hangar was one of the 32 planes caught in the ground when the 6th Armored Division, 3rd U.S. Army, captured the field, near Mülhausen, Germany. Stamped: "Passed for Publication. Field Press Censor. 10 APR 1945."

26

Labor Camps, POWs, and Grave Registration

One of the services that the army photographer had to do was grave registrations. I wondered when first going into service why they wanted to know if you had any scars or birthmarks or whether you had your appendix removed or something of this nature. I found out later that this was for identification, if you were killed in battle.

Many of our dead were so badly torn apart that they would call our signal company to send over a photographer to photograph anything that might help them to identify a body. This was not a duty that a photographer would look forward to, as you can well imagine.

Grave registration people would go out to collect the dead, and most of the time there would be dead soldiers everywhere. Many times some bodies had been there so long after battle before being picked up that the body was decomposed or had burst open. The odor was terrible and is something you never forget.

This job of grave registration was a sad and distasteful job, but someone had to do it.

Hitler had planned to build a super race that would rule the entire world. His dream of racial purity and total world domination ended when he took his own life. The one thing that did not die with Hitler was the memory of the millions that had died because of him. Had he looked back on history, he could have seen that many others had tried this and all had failed. Instead of power and pride, he had led the German people to defeat, destruction and shame. He had, however, come very close to conquering his part of the world.

Ben Franklin once said, "There was never a good war or never a bad peace." I have been back to Europe many times since the end of World War II, and the cities that were in rubble in 1945 have been rebuilt, with very little sign of the war ever having taken place. Even East Germany began to rebuild after the Berlin Wall came down, although some of the buildings in the smaller towns still show bullet holes and some signs of wartime destruction.

The prisoners of war had increased until, by the end of the war, we had thousands upon thousands of POWs here in the Unites States. They were brought back to the states to work on farms, roads or other areas that were non–war related, such as defense plants. They were paid 80 cents per day for this work and were treated well. They were well fed and were kept in warm, comfortable housing.

The Geneva Convention states that a prisoner of war should eat as well as the guards that guard him. Certainly the ones in the USA did eat well. Our soldiers in Germany were not treated so well, and they lived in unsanitary and uncomfortable stalags. Many of the Red Cross packages that they were supposed to receive never reached them, because both German civilians and soldiers stole them in many cases. Many of our soldiers did not receive proper medical attention while excellent medical attention was given to the German soldiers sent to the States.

One such German soldier who was captured and sent to the USA said that this was the best thing that ever happened to him during all his war service. He had never had it so good. He was safe, well-fed, well-housed, and he could save the money he made each day to take home with him when he returned to Germany after the war was over.

A captured German prisoner idles the time away under a lion monument in the town square of Lucka, Germany. He will soon be on his way to a 3rd U.S. Army Prisoner of War camp behind the lines. To the left is Charles Sumners' jeep. U.S. Army Signal Corps; photograph by C.E. Sumners. Stamped: "Passed for Publication. Field Press Censor. 18 APR 1945."

After the war was over, many of the slave laborers that were freed from the Germans were on the move going home. Russ Meyer and I entered a little town from which the Germans had retreated. Along with aid of some U.S. infantrymen, we opened up a guard-house and freed about 25 prisoners being held in this town.

They worked at a flour mill and a bakery that made bread for the German soldiers. The first thing they did, when we let them out of the enclosure where they had been locked up, was to knock the locks off the bakery and pass out the bread. I guess this was the first time they had been able to eat as much as they wanted in quite some time. They helped themselves to bread, flour and anything else that was edible. They also took as much as they could carry with them on their long march home.

166th Signal Photo Co., Det 16 Ornitz 23 APR 1945. This photograph shows the conditions and the amount of sleeping space for the prisoners at Buchenwald concentration camp. They range from young kids to old men, all doing the same amount of work each day.

166th Signal Photo Co., Det NR2 Moll 14 APR 1945. Bodies of the victims stacked in the building awaiting cremation in the large furnaces, specially built for such work. At the concentration camp at Weimar, Germany.

They came for the Communists,
　　and I didn't object ... for I wasn't a Communist.
They came for the Socialists,
　　and I didn't object ... for I wasn't a Socialist.
They came for the labor leaders,
　　and I didn't object ... for I wasn't a labor leader.
They came for the Jews,
　　and I didn't object ... for I wasn't a Jew.
Then they came for me ...
　　and there was no one left to object.
　　　　　　　　　　　　　　　—Martin Niemöller
　　　　　　　　　　　German Protestant Pastor, 1892–1984*

　　　Russ and I photographed a camp where there were about 300 young Jewish women that had been machined gunned to death in a field that was littered with dead bodies. Some of these women were half-dressed, and some of them would have been quite attractive. But they had been used as sex mates for the German SS officers and passed from

*http://www.verinet.com/~rwf/gi/gi5.html The website of Ron Fleischer.

166th Signal Photo Co., Det 10, Dougall 6 MAY 1945. Jewish women dead from brutality and malnutrition lying in the field awaiting burial by the civilians at the Hergenhein concentration camp, Germany.

166th Signal Photo Co., Det 16, Ornitz 23 APR 45. Bodies of the old men and young kids in the mass grave at the concentration camp near Buchenwald, Germany.

one camp to another. Finally, they were all housed at this location together, and the Germans were trying to destroy all the evidence about this. The soldiers had gunned them down in the field, but had not had time to bury them.

The Germans would usually dig a big ditch with a bulldozer and cover hundreds of these people all at one time. They would place others in a pit that looked something like a huge outdoor barbecue grill and burn them. When we arrived, there were some bodies lying by such a big pit, bodies which they had not had time to burn before we got there.

Another place we went to was a lake where the Germans had sunk hundreds of bodies to hide them. The GIs pumped the water out and made German civilians and soldiers dig the bodies out of the lake. What was left of these bodies was just mucklike flesh and bones, and the smell was awful.

When the Third Army liberated Buchenwald concentration camp, General Patton instituted the policy of forcing local German civilians to tour the camps and even help transport and bury the dead.

The German civilians *had* to have known what was going on, because you could smell those camps for miles before you reached them. You could always tell when you were getting near one of these areas by the stench. The odor of a dead decaying human being has a different, distinctive smell from any other smell I have ever encountered. But once you have smelled it, you will *never* forget it as long as you live.

166th Signal Photo Co., Det 10 Belfer 29 APR 1945. Civilians of the city of Nürnberg at the task of carrying the bodies of the slave laborers over the mile and a half stretch to the burial grounds.

We would go out and make pictures at these camps and then go back to the base to shower. You could wash our clothes in gasoline or burn them, but you could still smell that camp odor, and it stayed with you for some time.

166th Signal Photo Co., Det 10, Belfer 29 APR 25. Civilians of Nürnberg, both men and women, participate in the carrying of the bodies of the slave laborers a mile and a half outside the city of Nürnberg for burial.

It would be impossible for me to eat food for two or three days after being at one of these camps. It would take that much time for me to get all of that out of my system and to get back to eating and being normal. I tried to avoid as many of those assignments as possible because each time it just made me physically sick for days.

I often thought that if Hitler had used the same resources and the same energy in peaceful ventures that he used in war, Germany could have become a powerful nation without having to use war to accomplish those goals. If he had used these intelligent German people in science, medicine and industry, they could have done great things. The German scientists were so good in their field that, after the war, there was a race on by the American, British and Russians to get as many of them as they could to help with research.

If all of these people had devoted their time, their expertise and their know-how to things that would better mankind, rather than destroying mankind, what a blessing it could have been.

166th Signal Photo Co., Det 16 Ornitz 23 APR 1945. This tattoo was part of a man's body until it was skinned off by Nazi SS men and used as a decoration on the wall of their quarters, at Buchenwald concentration camp.

166th Signal Photo Co., Det 10 Belfer 29 APR 1945. At the burial grounds outside Nürnberg, Germany, a prayer was offered in English, Polish and German for the slave laborers who had been murdered by the Nazis.

27

CLOSE CALLS

Many soldiers in any war owe their lives to other soldiers. Some survive close calls because of fate — kismet — luck — prayer. Call it what you may. I know of many times when a split second made a difference in life or death; when suddenly you realize the tenuity of life and how precious is every breath drawn.

One example concerns Arthur Herz. He had gotten out of Germany, gone through Switzerland and Italy, and finally made it to the United States. He tried to join the air force, the navy and the marines, but was turned down. He was finally able to join the army as a photographer and was assigned to our company, the 166th.

Art was wounded in a German town toward the end of the war while he was talking to some of the local people. Since he spoke fluent German, he had been trying to talk the people into surrendering to the Americans to avoid more bloodshed. He was out in the street talking when a sniper shot him in the back.

Barney Caliendo was the photographer with him and knew that, if he went out to help his buddy Art, he would get shot also. So Caliendo pointed a pistol at a German civilian and told him to go get his buddy. The civilian was able to get Art out of the street, and they put him in a jeep and sent him back to an aid station. They were able to save him, and Arthur probably owes his life to Barney's taking the initiative and getting some fast action.

Barney Caliendo.

143

Charles "Porky" Atwell was a driver in one of our units. He was a large person—not tall, about 5'8", but he weighed about 230 pounds. Charley was hit with a large piece of shrapnel, and his back was just sliced open with a gash about six to eight inches long. Jim Ryan, another photographer, took his shirt off and actually held that gash together with his bare hands. He was able to slow, and almost stop, the bleeding until medics could get there. Chances are that this saved Atwell's life.

I have already mentioned my experience in Oberdorla, Germany, where the soldier was killed as he passed me. Was it blind luck or maybe the prayers of family and friends that kept me alive? Who knows? But that bullet didn't have my name on it.

We were in a jeep near the front lines on another occasion, when I was driving too fast and stirring up a lot of dust. The Germans started to shell in our direction, so I pulled off the road to get under cover of some kind. As soon as I stopped, we jumped out. Just as Lou Crabtree, our still man, stood up in the back to jump out, a shell came in and landed on the left side of the jeep about where he would have jumped. He froze there in the jeep. We all froze as we heard it land. It was a dud and did not explode. Had it exploded, I am certain that it would have killed Lou and possibly the rest of us.

Lou was never the same after that. He was older than the rest of us and could possibly see more danger than we could. His nerves were shot, and he was sent back to work in the company lab at headquarters for the rest of the war. Lou was the first of our group to pass away after we came back home. He died of cancer, not surviving long after he was diagnosed with it.

One time, we were parked in a little courtyard about 15 to 20 yards from the gate that was guarded by a soldier. We went inside for a while because it was cold. When we finally came back out, I cranked the jeep, but it went dead when I let out the clutch. I cranked it and started off again, and it went dead on me a second time. It had rolled back about 10 or 12 feet during all of this, and, just as it finally started up, a shell came in and landed right in the middle of that gate. That was just about where we would have been if the jeep had started the first time that I cranked it.

That shell killed the soldier guarding the gate and wounded two other soldiers there with him. No one thinks he's going to get killed—but, of course, many soldiers did.

One night I was taking our film back to the message center. The ground was covered with ice and snow, so I got my jeep in some ruts made by the half-tracks. Before I knew it, I had skidded about 25 or 30 yards on the under carriage of the jeep, and the tires were about four inches off the ground.

I was by myself at night, but you could see really well because of all the snow on the ground. I didn't know how I would be able to get my stuck jeep out, but I began to dig out around it as best I could. About that time, some soldiers came up in a truck, and they were able to pick the jeep up—one end at a time—and get it out of the ruts. I made sure not to follow half-track ruts from then on.

Actually, getting our film back at night was probably just as dangerous as going to the front lines to film the action. There were a lot of road guards all up and down the line going back to message center. Some of those guards were trigger-happy and would scare you to death. Sometimes you would hear that old bolt click on the carbine rifle *before* he asked for the password.

We had a lieutenant with us for a while who worked with the military government after the war was declared over. He was a good man and very smart. He spoke four or five languages, including German and French, and he was serving as an interpreter.

He was issued a vehicle with a driver, and they were on their way to work one day when they failed to hear the road guard tell them to stop. They continued to drive on, so the road guard opened up on them with a 50mm machine gun. The driver was not hit, but the lieutenant was killed.

It just seemed so unfair that he had lived through all the battles, only to be killed by friendly fire after the end of the war.

Once, my unit and I were in a convoy when I looked up and saw a German plane up ahead of us diving straight down for the convoy. I saw a road off to my left that went under a small railroad bridge. I cut off the main road in such a hurry that I scared the rest of the unit. Lieutenant Moore asked me, "Where in the hell are you going?" But by that time I was already stopped under the railroad bridge and two planes had made a couple of runs over our convoy.

They didn't do much damage to the convoy, but Lieutenant Moore said that my wild dash to get under cover was more frightening than the enemy planes.

One day we were going to the front lines after being at G-2 to look at the strategy maps to find out unit locations. Lieutenant Moore always thought that north was the way the jeep was pointed when we were trying to get directions.

We were going down this country road, and out from behind the bushes stepped an infantry sergeant. He said to us, "You better hold it there."

Lieutenant Moore then asked this sergeant, "Where is the point?" (The "point" was the most advanced position of our troops.)

The sergeant smiled and said, "Lieutenant, *you* are the point!"

Moore yelled, "Put it in reverse, Charlie. Let's get the hell out of here!"

At another time, we were with a convoy that was stopped when the

Soldiers advancing in France, surrounded by smoke from artillery and bombs, 1944. U.S. Army Signal Corps; photograph by C.E. Sumners. Stamped: "Confidential, Until Reclassified by Censor."

German planes came over strafing the area. We jumped out, and I crawled under the jeep. Lieutenant Moore and Joe Lapine got under a 2½-ton truck in front of me.

After the plane made a couple of passes and left, we got back in the jeep and Lieutenant Moore said, "Charlie, that jeep was not the best thing to get under in an air raid."

I replied, "It sure beats the hell out of that ammunition truck that you and Joe got under."

Moore almost fainted when he saw the sign on the back of that truck that read: "AMMUNITION Truck — Hazardous and Dangerous!"

28

SOUVENIRS

Souvenirs during the war were a big thing. We would pick up old German helmets, rifles, bayonets or any such German items relating to the war. When we went back to the rear company headquarters, which might be 40 or 50 miles behind the front lines, we would sell them to GIs located there. The German knives with the prized German logos emblazoned on the sides would bring $75 to $100 dollars each.

One of these knives that I picked up as a souvenir had engraved on the blade *Alle für Deutschland*. This was a dagger type of knife. We found at least 400 of these knives in boxes at a school and loaded them in the trailer behind the jeep.

I knew that Lieutenant Moore had wanted one of these knives so badly he could taste it, so I hung one of them on my belt when we got back to the company. When Moore saw that knife on my belt, his eyes got as big as saucers. He said to me, "I have to have that knife!"

I asked him what he would trade me for it. He traded me a pair of binoculars, a stopwatch and a camera for that one knife. After we made the trade, I took him out and showed him that we had about 75 more just like it still in the trailer behind the jeep. We sold the ones we kept for $50 to $75 dollars each.

I got my Luger pistol surprisingly and unexpectedly. It occurred just outside the little German town of Labits, located approximately 20 miles south of Leipzig. After cutting the Leipzig-Chemnitz autobahn, a task force composed of the 69th Tank Battalion and 44th Armored Infantry Battalion caught a company of German infantry retreating toward Leipzig. The Germans made no attempt to surrender, and the GIs had no alternative but to cut them down.

We halted our jeep near two fallen German soldiers, both quite obviously dead. One had been hit in the head with a .50 caliber round; the other had no visible wound. Meyer and I took several photos of the tanks and half-tracks passing by with the dead Germans in the foreground.

Suddenly, I thought I saw one of the figures move. I called Meyer's attention to it and went over to investigate. Since Russ could speak a little German, we hit upon a plan. Quite audibly, I drew and cocked my 45 pistol. Meyer said in German, "This first soldier is not dead. Come here and shoot him in the head."

That did the trick. The apparently dead Nazi jumped to his feet begging for his life and yelling, "Kamerad!"

Net proceeds—one Nazi POW and one Luger pistol.

Many soldiers sent home a lot of things from the war. One of the men in my company liked grandfather clocks, and he sent home more than you can imagine. He would take them apart and send them home in huge packages, planning to reassemble them after the war.

I did not send home a lot of things, but I did send home to my youngest brother Bob an opera hat with a collapsible top—a tall black hat used in stage plays. I also sent him an Iron Cross that I had actually taken off a dead German soldier and a German officer's dagger with an impressive scabbard that had Nazi symbols on it.

I don't know what happened to these prized souvenirs, but he had them for several years. He was about twelve years old at the time and took them to school to show them to his classmates.

29

War Ends in Europe

On the 7th of May, Lieutenant Moore and I decided to go to the town of Reims, France. He had just found out that his brother Fred, who was General Eisenhower's personal photographer, was going to be at the headquarters.

As we approached Reims, an M.P. stopped us outside the building. We then saw a large officer's car drive up, and German officers got out of it. We thought this was very strange and wondered why they were way back here since, as far as we knew, the war was still going on back up front.

It was not until the next day that we found out what had taken place that day. This was the day General Eisenhower and General Jodl and the Russians signed the unconditional surrender terms in Reims. We were there loaded with cameras, but we couldn't get in to make a picture. Furthermore, we didn't even get to see Lieutenant Moore's brother, Fred.

So, the war ended in Europe May 7, 1945.

While we were awaiting orders, I learned that my brother Paul was with the 809th Tank Destroyer Battalion with the Second Armored Division located near Pilsen, Czechoslovakia. I went to Third Army Headquarters and got Lieutenant Threlkel to give me a jeep and cut orders to have me attached to the Second Armored Division's public relations department.

When I got to Pilsen, however, I found out that Paul's outfit had left that morning headed home to the States, and I missed see-

Eisenhower at Reims — Allied force leaders at the signing. National Archives, courtesy of Franklin D. Roosevelt Library Digital Archives. May 7, 1945.

German officers sign unconditional surrender in Reims, France. National Archives, courtesy of Franklin D. Roosevelt Library Digital Archives. May 7, 1945.

Band of 18th Tank Battalion, 8th Armored Division, XXII Corps, 3rd U.S. Army, plays at Club Tobasco, enlisted men's club for men of XXII Corps, 3rd U.S. Army, near Pilsen, Czechoslovakia. Soldiers enjoy company of Czechoslovakian women at club. The only club for enlisted men in this vicinity, the club was organized by the 18th Tank Battalion. U.S. Army Signal Corps; photograph by C.E. Sumners. Stamped: "Passed for Publication 26, June, 1945."

Soldiers enjoy company of Czechoslovakian women in beer garden of Club Tobasco near Pilsen, Czechoslovakia. U.S. Army Signal Corps; photograph by C.E. Sumners. Stamped: "Passed for Publication. 26 JUN 1945."

ing him by about six hours. We had not seen each other in nearly three years, even though we were both in the same part of the world an ocean away from home.

I stayed in Pilsen for about two weeks. They had a photo section in this Second Armored, and everyday I got assignments with the public relations department. I would photograph generals decorating soldiers, ceremonies honoring those killed in battles and all types of such assignments. For four or five days I was doing all the work, and the others would just stand around and watch. Finally, I told them I had to go back to my company, because I was a high-point man and was due to go home.

I had my own jeep and a card signed by General Eisenhower that allowed me to go anywhere I wanted to go without anyone questioning me. So, I went over to the Club Tobasco, a hotel located on Lake Tobasco, and stayed there a few days. That was a beautiful lake, and they had a big party and dance each night. I would swim each day in the lake and go dancing every night in the nightclub.

I met a very pretty girl, but she could speak little English. I certainly couldn't speak her language, but we had a lot of fun swimming, dancing and eating at the club. I finally decided that I had better get on back to my company before someone found out where I was and what I had been doing. So, I headed back to a place below Munich, Germany, and was able to locate our company.

30

MEMORY BANK STORIES

As a Signal Corps "still photographer" with General George Patton's Third Army during World War II, I made many combat pictures of many things. Some of my photographs were published in U.S. newspapers and the *Stars and Stripes*. I don't remember a lot of my photos, but some I *do* remember — vividly!

Some of the pictures that I do remember *most* are ones I did *not* take, but are pictures that are mirrored in my memory bank. They seem to be there permanently, and they emerge as graphic images anytime I think of the war or when things come along, as they often do, to remind me.

One of these pictures I didn't take that is still in my memory bank is one of an old Frenchman standing in the middle of the street with his hat off, his gray hair blowing in the wind and tears running down his cheeks. In the street in front of him were the broken pieces of his wagon and his horse lying there kicking his last kick — killed by the shrapnel of an exploding shell.

The old man was not hurt, but, since I had grown up on a farm, I knew what the loss of his horse meant to him. He probably had also lost the use of his farmhouse already to both the Germans first and then the Allies. His fields where he grew his crops had possibly been mined or the crops destroyed by this war. And here — on this street — his horse lay dying and he stood crying.

We put a rope around the horse's head and pulled it out of the street so our convoy could get through. We also pushed the old wagon with its broken shafts over into a ditch … and we left them there.

A day or so later, I came back through that little town. The wagon was still in the ditch, but all that was left of the horse was his head and his hoofs with part of the legs. The rest had been cut out and probably eaten by the hungry French people.

There were many people who had nothing to eat and went hungry for several days. The Germans had stripped them bare of food and supplies when they had come through,

French town, 1944. Soldiers coming up the hill. Later this old horse was dead on side of the road. Photograph by C.E. Sumners.

and it was a while before the Americans could get food to them. They would certainly eat horse meat or about anything else they could get their hands on. It was agonizing to see the hunger on the faces of those people — especially the small children and the old folks.

Another picture that I have in my bank of memories was of an American soldier taking a young German woman into a barn, against her wishes. She came out after five or ten minutes straightening her skirt, and she ran down the street crying.

I don't know: possibly, if I had tried to stop this, I would have had to kill him or he would have had to kill me — one or the other. I have always felt bad that I had not done anything to stop this. Yet, on the other hand, I also thought of the German women that I had seen in the prisoner of war camps. They would take off their blouses and bras and shake their breasts at the guards outside. I thought, "Who am I to judge?" and that was my rationalization for letting this happen without at least trying to stop it.

Nevertheless, I still remember it, and I must have felt guilty about it. The image remains.

Another picture that I didn't take is one burned into my memory when we were in Belgium during the Battle of the Bulge. We had moved into an empty house for a day or so. It was cold, there was snow on the ground, and miserable weather conditions were all around us.

One morning, I went outside and walked behind an old shed, or smokehouse. Behind this old building were four people: a woman, her husband and two kids—a boy and a girl. They were, lying there — dead in the snow — huddled together with the woman and man trying to cover the children's bodies with their own.

About six or eight feet away was a crater in the ground, made by a mortar shell that had exploded. I do not know how long they had been there, but their bodies were frozen and were pretty well covered with snow. I had no way of knowing if the shell was from the German guns or ours.

I did not take a picture of this, but I still remember this whole family huddled there and covered with snow — a father trying to shield his family from the enemy.

One of the most vivid of my memories is a scene I mentioned earlier. A tank had taken a direct hit in a wooded area not too far from where Russ Meyer and I were located. The guy got out of the tank, rolled off the side of it kind of sideways and staggered toward us.

In a few short minutes, he was dead at our feet. His body was full of shrapnel, from his neck down, and the blood bubbling out of him covered the snow where he lay.

I still remember his words, this dying soldier, and they will always be with me: "No, God. Not me. Not me, God, not me."

Very few people today even think about World War II, as we have had the Korean War, Vietnam, the Gulf War and other conflicts since then. We have had other things to take our minds off horror like this, and thus we shove the pictures to the back of our mind. There is still no World War II memorial, but I understand that work is being done to get this monument built. Maybe sometime during my lifetime we will have a memorial to honor the soldiers that fought and died in this war.

Meanwhile, these are things you remember. And when, from time to time, you see war movies like *Saving Private Ryan* and other war movies or history documentaries on TV, a flash of these memories come flooding back — the *real* movies. It then takes a while to get these thoughts out of your mind as you remind yourself that, "It's all over and done with and it happened a long time ago."

But the memory bank never really closes.

31

WILD BAD KREUTH

After the war was over in Europe, we were sent to Wild Bad Kreuth to wait for transportation to get us back to the coast so that we could get on a ship going back to the States. Wild Bad Kreuth is about 30 miles from Munich, Germany, in the foothills of the Alps. Our "barracks" had actually been a health resort before the war (the German word, "bad," means "spa") and there were flowing springs behind these barracks. This was a beautiful place with a wide-open meadow in front of it and the mountains behind.

Many of the soldiers had gone out and found old German autos, motorcycles and motor bikes, and even some beautiful horses. There were stables where the horses could be kept. I don't know where they got the horse feed, but they probably took fodder as they pleased, as we were allowed to do so since we were the "conquering heroes."

One day, Lieutenant Elk decided to show everyone how to ride a horse, so he took this big mare out of the stable. She was an impressive looking red horse with a white blaze on her forehead and white stocking feet. He trotted her out to the other side of the meadow and came back as fast as that horse could run. Suddenly, she stepped in a hole, and Lieutenant Elk went airborne for about 20 feet. He landed on his shoulder and broke it, which put him in the hospital. After that, an order came down that all the confiscated cars, motorcycles, motorbikes and horses must be removed.

We had time on our hands, so we

Photograph on front of small poster about "Restaurant — Touristenstube — Health Resort" in Wild Bad Kreuth, Bavaria. American soldiers billeted here waiting to return home after World War II. 1945.

155

Men of 166th Signal Photo Company, just recently awarded the Bronze and Silver Star awards. L-R: Cpl. Charles E. Sumners, Sgt. Bill Teas, Sgt. Ted Sizer, Sgt. Mike Marder, Sgt. Russell Meyer, Sgt. Bill Tompko. Wild Bad Kreuth, Germany. Photograph by Lou Dorman, June 1945.

Men of the 166th Signal Photo Company receiving awards. Presented by Chief Signal Officer, Col. E.F. Hammond, 3rd U.S. Army at Wild Bad Kreuth, Germany, June 1945. U.S. Army Signal Corps; photograph by Don English.

would go deer hunting with a Thompson submachine gun. I still can't believe that I missed a deer standing in the middle of a creek shooting with a submachine gun, but I sure did. We would go fishing with hand grenades. We would see some fish, throw a grenade into the stream and jump behind a tree as it went off.

You must remember that these were men that had been in combat for a long time, and that we would only fall out of formation to go where they kept the big kegs of beer or to eat.

One day several of us were sitting around, and we could see the snow and the snow line up there on the mountains. Someone said there was a road going up there that was possibly used when the German ski troopers were training in this location. So, six of us decided to take the road up the mountain to make a snowball. We thought it was only about four or five miles up there, but in reality, it was more like ten miles; but we didn't care.

We were walking along this road talking and making noise. Of course, we did not take our guns with us because the war was over, and we saw no need to carry this extra load up a mountainside. About five miles up the road, we saw an old cabin up on the left side of the road.

We got to within 25 or 30 yards when suddenly the door flew open, and several Ger-

L–R: Ted Sizer; John Blankenhorne; Russ Meyer; Mike Marder; Walter Snowden. Members of 166th Signal Photo Co. relaxing at Wild Bad Kreuth, Bavaria, while waiting to ship back to U.S.A. 1945. Photograph by Gene Abrams.

man soldiers came out through the door. They were still in their German uniforms and
still had their rifles. They ran up the mountain, and we ran down the mountain at the
same time — all of us scared to death!

**Wild Bad Kreuth. Members of 166th Signal Photo Co. were billeted here in 1945 awaiting
transportation home. Photograph taken on Sumners' visit back to Europe in 1977.**

These Germans were probably some of the Hitler-Jugends who had not surrendered.
There were several of these groups of young Germans that had continued to snipe and
go out on raids at night. So it was safer to stay down there with the company. That incident, of course, ended our snowball party.

Lieutenant Moore was my unit commanding officer, and after a while he more or
less gave Russ Meyer and me free reign to set our schedule to go where we wanted to go
and do what we wanted to do to get action combat pictures. Many times, Lieutenant
Moore did not even know where we were. When we got back from shooting our pictures,
we would check in with him to let him know what we had been doing.

I was, of course, quite fond of Lieutenant Moore who was almost old enough to be
my father. Meyer was less so as he always resented authority, and to him Lieutenant
Moore was authority. Russ just did not like anyone telling him what he could and could
not do.

Lieutenant Moore always had two goals for us, he said. One was to make the best
combat pictures that we could possibly take, and we did that. The other goal, which he
said was more important, was that all of us in his unit get home alive. He accomplished
that goal as well. Of the 11 people in that unit, there are only four of us that are still alive
today. But, we all came back from the war alive — some had a few scratches, but no one
had any serious wounds of any kind.

Weekly paper published by 166th Signal Photo Company, 3rd U.S. Army. A notice in 2nd column announces that "men of the 166th are now authorized FIVE Battle Stars for their ETO Ribbons." U.S. Army Signal Corps.

After the war was over, all the older men were sent home first, even before those men with high rotation points. Lieutenant Moore was set to be shipped home, so he called the unit together and made a good-bye speech to us. He thanked all of us and told us that he had appreciated all the work we had done.

A few hours later, I was walking across the company area and heard someone call my name. I looked around, and it was Lieutenant Moore. He had on his Class A uniform and was all shaved up and looked like an officer ready to go home. He had a big grin on his face as he came up to speak to me. He said, "Charlie, I just wanted to say a special good-bye to you."

I did not know whether to salute him or what, so I stepped up and held out my hand. He brushed my hand aside and gave me a big hug. As I looked at him, tears were running down his cheeks, and I knew then and there that this old soldier was just a really softhearted man.

I continued to stay in touch with him after the war, and I still have several letters that he wrote me before he died. He was a tough old soldier whom I truly admired, and I am thankful that I had an officer like that who allowed Meyer and me the freedom to make combat pictures the way we were able to.

32

GOING HOME AND AFTERMATH

Going home after the war was not a pleasant experience. Russ Meyer and I had a high point total for going home, because we had both been there a long time and had five battle stars for being in five major campaigns. You got a certain amount of points for each campaign, for length of service, for combat time and for medals. I had the Bronze Star and various other awards, so I had enough points for rotation. The older men had already left. We left the company and were put with an artillery outfit near Verdun. We were supposed to fly home, but the planes we were to go on were taken over by a group flying refugees back to Algeria. We had to stay with that artillery outfit for a while, and then they moved us down to those tent cities along the coast near Marseille, France.

I stayed at several tent cities—Camp Camel, Camp Lucky Strike and Camp New Orleans. By November, my company was already back in the States, and I—with more rotation points—had still not left for home. They finally formed us into packets according to states' names. So I left France with a group of about 25 GIs from Alabama, and we were the only troops on board.

They put us on an old victory ship that was in bad need of repair. The ship had come from the States loaded with toilet paper, 2½-ton trucks and other cargo, and now they were just turning it around and sending it back without unloading all that cargo. It was in such bad condition that they

Arriving at tent city — Camp New Orleans, France, 1945. Awaiting transportation back to U.S.A. Charles Sumners, with helmet, center beyond steering wheel of second jeep others unidentified.

161

knew it would not make it across the North Atlantic, so they dispatched us on a southern route. In fact, we were 19 days on the ocean coming back home.

We had to stop in Gibraltar because a German POW had stowed away in one of the trucks. After a couple of days out, he got hungry and thirsty and gave himself up. Several in my group grabbed him and would have thrown him overboard, but the captain and some of the crew stopped them before they could toss him in the ocean. So, we were in Gibraltar a couple of days while negotiations went on between the ship's captain and the British port authorities to decide what to do about the stowaway. The kid only had one hand as the Russians had cut off the other. So he was trying to get away from the Russians and the Germans and get to America for a better life.

We finally left and it was slow going. On the night before Thanksgiving Day, they had told us we were going to be fed the traditional Thanksgiving dinner of turkey, dressing and cranberry sauce with mashed potatoes and bread. Oh, you never heard such a wonderful menu! It sounded so good, and we were really looking forward to this meal. The cooks got the frozen turkeys out and thawed them, but they were as black as jets and smelled awful. They were thrown overboard, and we had cold cuts. I guess the sharks got our Thanksgiving dinner.

Somewhere in the middle of the ocean, they shut down all the engines and worked on them for 24 hours. They finally got the engines going again, and we limped into New York. We were on that ship for 19 days, when a nine or ten-day trip on the North Atlantic route was normal. We landed in Fort Hamilton on December 5, 1945 and were there for a few days of processing.

I came home with a soldier from Birmingham, Alabama, and he said he was going to do two things while he was in New York before going home. He was going to call his wife in Birmingham to tell her he was on his way home, and then he was going to get himself a bottle of whiskey.

Well, he got his bottle of whiskey, and he and I went out to a telephone booth to put in his call. The operator told him that all circuits were busy at that time, but, as soon as she could get his call through, she would call him back at that number. So, we sat there for about an hour with him sipping on this whiskey. When the call finally came through, I had to answer the phone to talk to his wife.

I told her that he had gone back inside for some more processing, but that he was in the States and would be getting home soon. I didn't tell her that he was so drunk he couldn't get up off the bench in order to talk with her.

Some 20 years later, I was in Sears in Birmingham when a man came up to me and said that he would know me anywhere. Realizing that I did not recognize him, he said, "You don't recognize me because I have lost all of my hair. My name is Cook, and you are the guy that talked to my wife in New York when I was so drunk I couldn't get up to talk to her."

Of course, I remembered him then. We talked for a while and have never run into each other again, even though we both lived in Birmingham for a long time.

Many of the returning veterans had problems—some psychological, some with wrestling to "get off the bottle." Many of them blamed their drinking and drug problems on the war and the military, but I do not agree with them.

When I first came home after the war, I had trouble just sitting still. For years, you have been "on a roll" or "on a high," as in war everything is fast-paced and exciting. Suddenly you are going at a slow pace with peace and quietness of home and nothing much to do other than attend a movie or such.

It takes a while to get your nerves back to the point where you can sit still and handle this slow-paced life that you were used to before the war. I had trouble sometimes at night. I would wake up in a cold sweat, not realizing for a moment where I was or what was going on.

I finally decided that I would use the GI Bill and go to college. Joe Carr and I went down to Auburn University to enroll. My high school at Vincent, Alabama, had burned while I was in service and there were no records to have sent to the registrar. I asked Mr. D.B. Smith, the principal, to help me with the needed records, and he gave me a report card that I am sure was better than the one I had really earned at school.

I was sitting there at Auburn with a large group waiting to enroll, and I got really nervous just waiting. I told Joe that I would wait for him outside, and that maybe by next quarter I would be ready to handle college. Joe enrolled and later graduated from Auburn, but I was just not quite ready to sit still for classes at that time.

A friend of mine was in an armored division driving a tank, and he had four or five tanks shot out from under him. He came home and seemed to be okay for years and years. However, when Desert Storm came up and they were showing the tank battles on television, it brought back memories that he could not put aside. He wouldn't see anyone and didn't want any visitors or anyone to talk to him. He would go into his bedroom and close the door, and he would go into that shell for weeks at a time.

Another friend had been an infantry captain and had lost about all of his company in the Battle of the Bulge. This caused him to have a lot of problems later. His father owned a heating and air-conditioning company in Birmingham, Alabama. It was a good business that was growing, so the father retired and turned it over to his son. After two years, it was in bankruptcy as the son had "hit the bottle" and gambled until the business failed. He lost his wife and family. The last I heard from him he had left Birmingham, and no one seemed to know what had happened to him.

For some of the veterans who came back, the war was not over. In many cases, other battles were just starting for them as they had a terrible time adjusting. One fellow I knew had a wife and two children. He was about 35 years old and making good money with a job as a welder at U.S. Steel. But he just could not leave the bottle alone and he would get drunk every weekend. Finally, he wound up with cirrhosis of the liver and died about five years after coming home.

Even as scary and horrible as the war was, it had its good points also. Take me, for instance. I had never been out of Alabama and knew nothing about the world or people of other cultures and religions. I was just out of high school and didn't know a lot of things.

I had never been around anyone who was homosexual. I had heard of it, but I didn't even believe it to be a fact.

When we were in Ireland, I had a lieutenant tell me to go down to the motor pool and get a jeep. He wanted me to drive him into Bangor, which was a fairly large city.

T/5 Charles Sumners, 166th Signal Photo Co., U.S. Army — a wiser man by the end of the war than the teenager who left home for bootcamp.

We drove in, stopped at a large hotel, and went into a beautiful restaurant. We had a very fancy meal with lace tablecloth, linen napkins, finger bowls, a bottle of wine and a fancy dessert. I did not realize at that time that he was courting me — that's how naive I was then.

Several days later, I was on guard duty. This same lieutenant was officer of the day, which meant he was in charge of the guards. There was a big room at the castle where the guards waiting to go on duty stayed, and there was a smaller room next to it where the officer of the day stayed. This room had a bed and a fireplace.

Well, the lieutenant told me that when I posted my 12:00 relief, I was to come to his room and check on his fire. He said I would possibly need to put some more wood on by that time. I still didn't think anything was strange about this, so I went in and "chunked" his fire.

I looked over and he was in the bed. There was a nightstand by the bed with a fifth of Scotch and two glasses. The bottle was about two inches or so empty, and he told me to pour myself a drink. I replied, "I'm sorry, Sir, but I'm on guard duty, and that's not allowed."

He said, "Don't worry about that. I'm officer of the day. Here, I'll pour you a drink." He then threw the covers back to get up to pour my drink, and he was as naked as a jaybird!

I said, "I believe I heard one of my guards call me, and I've got to check on them." I got out of there as fast as I could.

I heard that he was later caught and kicked out of the service for his conduct. This was a strange thing, as the man was brilliant, an excellent still photographer, and a good officer in many other respects. I found out later that he had tried to have me transferred into his unit, but our Lt. Moore had refused the transfer.

I came home a wiser man than the teenager who had left.

33

REUNIONS

There were 11 people in my newsreel unit in Europe during World War II. Of these, only four are still alive: Russ Meyer and Harry Downard live in California, Bob Brill lives in New Jersey, and I live in Alabama.

Lieutenant Moore was our officer. After the war, he was involved in the motion picture industry in California. He died about five years ago, well past the age of 80.

Lou Crabtree was the first to pass away, dying of cancer about five years after the war was over. Gordon Patmon died sometime later.

Ralph Butterfield was a teacher at Riverside Community College in California and edited a book called *Patton's GI Photographers*. Ralph was a fine man, a good friend and one of the most disciplined human beings that I have ever known. He always smoked a pipe, but he would only have one pipe each day — after dinner — and that was the only time. He was a very exacting person who would measure the depth and temperature of a pool before he would jump in for a swim. Russ Meyer, Homer Foreman and I went fishing with Ralph at one of the lakes near his home not long before he died. It was a wonderful visit.

Harry Downard was one of the movie cameramen in my unit and another good friend of mine. His first wife died many years after the war and he later remarried. He and his wife live in California today and are in pretty good health. He is past 80 years old but is still active and enjoys life.

Bob Brill lives in New Jersey. I have not seen Bob in several years, but he attended many of our reunions. Bob was a movie cameraman in our outfit, but he was loaned out to other units for several assignments since they were short of men in this area.

Joe Lapine was a still photographer with our outfit and later was elected mayor of his town. He was an outstanding man, a great human being, but not the best soldier in the world. He was a good photographer, but his nerves sometimes could not stand the rigors of being a combat photographer. He just couldn't take it; he'd go all to pieces.

Charles Sullivan was an excellent still photographer and a good guy. He was redheaded and a snappy dresser. He was a typical fellow from New York, but he and this son of the South got along well together.

Gene Abrams was a paper salesman after the war. He was a terrific fellow and attended many of our reunions. Russ, Gene and I made a trip back to Europe together and had a great time revisiting many of the places where we had been during the war.

Russ Meyer went home to California and became a noted Hollywood producer and director of some 25 films. Russ is still alive, although he is not in good health. I made a visit out to see him in August 2000 and spent a few days with him.

Russ was more or less responsible for keeping our group of people together through the years. This group was basically the brothers he never had. For example, he would send me an airline ticket and say, "Come out. I want to see you." He would do this with several of the guys who maybe didn't have the money for transportation to go to the places wherever we were having our reunion. He would send them a ticket, and I'm sure they appreciated his making sure that they were there. If he were ever in a town where any of the guys lived, he would stop by and see them, take them out to dinner, so on.

Each year, due to Meyer's efforts, members of the 166th have met at reunions at Camp Crowder in Neosho, Missouri, and other parts of the country. Through the years, the large group has dwindled to a very few who are alive and able to travel. In 1999, we did not meet.

Time goes by, we get older and memories fade. The war we lived through is ancient history to the young students of today. But the facts remain, and those for whom we tell these stories will perhaps store them in a memory bank and remember those of us who lived them.

Reunion of 166th Photo Company. Seated: John Marshall, Kenny Parker, Orville Hallberg, Bud Musae, Fred Mandell, Carlton White, Dick Simon, Billy Newhouse. Center bending: Lt. Gene Moore. Standing first row: Sammy Senninburg, Harry Downard, Paul Fox, Lou Connell, "Red" Bryson, Russ Meyer, Lou Dorman, Jim Ryan, unidentified. Back row: Ralph Butterfield, Gene Abrams, Fred Owens, Eve Meyer.

34

RUSS MEYER

Any person who has been in any branch of the military, especially if combat were involved, will understand why it is important to elaborate a wee bit on Russ Meyer. We were buddies, "stubborn-mates" and comrades in arms. As the reader has seen, we shared many hours together seeing, experiencing and recording memories of exciting, momentous, scary, even horrendous events. We were friends who understood each other and respected each other's individuality.

So, I share with you …

The army needed photographers, so back in 1942 the motion picture industry in California came to an agreement with the federal government. If the government would leave their photographers alone, they would conduct training classes for several groups of people for the army. They would give these people film and a camera to go out and take pictures. If they were learning movies, they would shoot a little scene; if it were stills, they would make still photographs.

Meyer went to one of these schools, and this is how he came to be an army photographer. He and all the guys that went to these schools came out as sergeants.

Russ was born March 21, 1922, in California. He was not born with a silver spoon in his mouth. His early days were struggles because his mother and father divorced. He had one sister, Lucinda. His mother remarried, and he got along pretty well with his stepfather, but he struck out on his own when he was about 17 years old.

I don't know if Russ ever finished high school, but he was a smart, strong-willed and determined young man. Later on, he lectured at some of the finest colleges in the United States, England and France. You would never know that he did not have any formal training by listening to him speak or seeing some of his work.

When I first met him in Camp Crowder, we had nothing in common. Russ was just another soldier, and I guess I was just another GI as far as he was concerned. With 150 people in your outfit, you didn't really get close to many and then possibly just the ones you bunked next to or happened to work with. Since I was in the motor pool and he was in a camera school or doing something related to photography, we just did not see that much of each other at that time.

But once we were formed into a unit and we were together, there seemed to be a bond of friendship that grew daily. Finally after we were overseas, we had three or four still photographers and the same number of movie men in our unit. He looked around at the still photographers and said, "I'm not going into combat with these people." Then he looked at me and said, "I'm going with you. I'm going to teach you photography, and you will be a still photographer."

So, he took me aside and we went through this and that, and he showed me everything that he thought I needed to know. I never considered myself a great photographer, but if you were up there where the action was going on — and there was action everywhere — then you just had to point the camera, click the shutter and make a combat picture. I could always depend on him to tell me what the light was, because he had the light meter out checking it every 30 minutes.

Russ was very exact in everything he did. That is the reason that some of his combat films were the best of anyone in our company or anywhere. He was totally unaware of anything other than what he was doing when he was filming. He would always say, "be sure you get the right exposure and be sure you shoot enough film. Tie it all together and have continuity between your long shots and your inserts, closeups, etc."

In combat you did not get too many closeups. I sure did not want many closeups!

Russ always resented authority and did not want a lot of people telling him what to do or how to do it. He always knew what he wanted to do, and he knew how to do it. A good example of this was when we first landed in France and moved into a little bivouac area. He loaded his musette bag with film, got his camera and headed out to the front. He just could not wait to get up there and make combat pictures.

He was gone for about two days before he ran out of film, so he came back in to get more. Lt. Moore ordered him not to leave again, and told him, "We were worried sick about you and didn't know where you were. We thought you might be dead." This made Russ mad, but he had to follow orders.

Finally he talked them into letting us go with the First Army. So Russ, Abrams, another still photographer and I left with the First Army and had assignments in the little towns before you get to St. Lô. We were attached to the 30th and 28th Infantry divisions, but I don't recall any armored division until we were attached to Patton's Third Army.

Russ was determined to be a success and told me on many occasions that he planned to be wealthy in civilian life. He said, "I am going to have money and do not intend to have to buy anything on credit." He resented the fact that when he was in school, his family had to buy groceries from a little neighborhood grocery store on credit. He attended school with the son of the owner of the grocery store, and Russ always felt humiliated knowing that this kid knew that his family owed money to this kid's family.

He said, "I am going to be famous. I'm going to be rich, and I'm not going to have to ask anyone for anything. I'm going to be the one telling other people what to do and not having them tell me what to do."

When Russ was discharged from the service, he was still interested in photography work. He took a job with some lumber outfit for a while and then worked for a railroad doing some films and such work. He always wanted that camera handy at all times. He was married to several beautiful women and lived with quite a few others. All these women would probably tell you that his first love was photography and his second love was his old army buddies. He would go to great lengths to see them and keep that friendship alive, for we were the brothers he never had.

Russ and I became very close friends, and he relied on me for a lot of things, but I also relied on him for anything that had to do with photography. To me he was the very best photographer ever, and he proved that later on when he started making movies. He wanted me to go to California with him after the war, but I told him that all I wanted to do was go home. I did not care anything about a career with photography. I told him all I wanted was getting this damn war over with and going back home.

Meyer's movies were not the kind that you would show at your PTA, but if you looked at them from a technical standpoint, you would see that they were perfection. The exposure, the scenes and the length of the scenes were to perfection. He would take bartenders, waitresses, taxi drivers and some of his old army buddies and make movies with them. Most of these people had never even

Russ Meyer with Arriflex camera.

been in a high school play before, but he was so good that he could make movies with these nonprofessional people.

Russ and I have gone back to Europe several times and retraced our steps from the beaches all the way to the Berlin Wall. There was no wall during the war, and of course now there is no evidence that the wall ever existed — it's just completely gone. The last couple of times we were over there, we were able to go on into several of the towns in the East Zone. We went to Oberdorla, Leipzig and a lot of little towns that we went through during the war before we met up with the Russians. It was good to finally be able to go back to those places.

35

BACK TO EUROPE

Passport

My first trip back to Europe was in 1977, and I had a terrible time trying to get a passport. I did not have a birth certificate since I was delivered by a midwife, and there was never any birth recorded anywhere. This was a common custom in the rural South in those days.

I tried many ways to get a birth certificate, to no avail. I even wrote to the census bureau in Kansas City, Missouri, but still had no luck. I then carried my mother and Aunt Alva, my mother's sister, to the State Bureau of Vital Statistics in Montgomery, Alabama, and they swore affidavits that I was Charles E. Sumners and that this was my correct age. I still could not get a birth certificate.

Finally, someone found a school record in the courthouse in Columbiana, Alabama, which was the county seat of Shelby County. This record showed that I had made the highest grade on an achievement test when I was in the third grade. So I got all my material ready and sent it to a friend in Miami, Florida, where passports were issued at that time. She took this information to the office and told them that Charles Sumners was to leave for Europe soon and needed this passport quickly. They issued me a temporary passport, good for 90 days. Later on, I was able to get a regular passport.

I've often wondered about the irony of this experience. I had a driver's license, a Social Security number, and a marriage certificate. I had my mother and aunt vouch for me that I was a person and not a ghost. The army had drafted me, trained me, fed and clothed me, sent me to Europe (GI class), and discharged me. Yet it was my third grade scholastics that "made" me official! I've heard that one has to have a birth certificate in order to be certified dead. I guess that means I could live forever.

I left out of Birmingham, Alabama, on Delta, flying to New York for the first leg of my trip. It was a beautiful day with not a cloud in the sky, but we ran into some turbulence along the way. I was seated in the tail end of the plane, and, by the time we landed in New York, I was sick as a horse. If I could have found a bus station, I probably would have crawled on a bus and gone back home. During the three-hour layover, I walked around the airport and drank a couple of cokes.

I felt much better by the time I got on the plane, and I was seated next to a nice Jewish lady who could speak a little English. I couldn't speak German, but we managed to communicate enough to handle the situation. She and her husband were separated during the war, and both were sent to different work camps. She made German soldiers' uniforms in a labor camp, and her husband did labor jobs in his camp.

They did not see each other for over three years, but miraculously got together when the war ended. They did not have any money, and the only clothes they had were those they were wearing. They were lucky that they had some friends in the United States who had some money and helped them get back into business. They got into the leather goods business, making purses, wallets, jackets, leather coats, so on. They now owned a large store in London, one in Canada, and a huge place in Munich, Germany.

When I told her where we were staying, she said that it was one of the nicest hotels in Munich and that she would have her chauffeur drive me there if my friend did not meet me at the airport. I told her, "Surely your husband will be coming to meet you."

She said, "Oh no, he has to stay and take care of the business." Of course, my friend was there to meet me, but the trip to Munich was enjoyable because of this experience with this gracious survivor.

Russ asked me to take another trip back to Germany with him, and one purpose was so he could buy a big Arriflex camera from Arnold & Richter. He purchased this camera and shot film over there for about ten days. Buying the camera in Germany saved him enough money (over what it would have cost him in the states) to pay for both our trips there. So he saved money, and we also had a great time together.

We drove through Germany back to the beaches in France. Then we retraced our steps from Utah Beach all the way through Germany, as we had traveled in the battles of World War II. We went through many of the towns where we had filmed, such as St. Lô, Avranches, Reims and Paris.

We went all the way into Wild Bad Kreuth, Germany, in the foothills of the Alps, where we had been billeted. This is a beautiful place where we had stayed about one month at the end of the war awaiting a boat to take us home. It was here that medal ceremonies were held for the 166th Signal Photo Company.

We tried while we were in Paris to find Mrs. Suthro. She is the lady who shared her home with us our first night in Paris after its liberation. She was a sociable, pretty lady, and her husband was a Free French colonel. Their son, who was about 12 years old at the time, has restored the same house and now lives in it.

We visited with the Uriet family in Jarney with whom we had stayed a couple of times during the war. The last time was just

Charles Sumners in front of a hedgerow in France. Photograph taken on a visit back to Europe in 1977.

Charles Sumners and Russ Meyer at Wild Bad Kreuth on trip back to Europe in 1977. This was a German Ski Trooper Barracks. Alps in the background. U.S. Troops were there in June–July 1945, waiting for transportation home after the war was over.

before the Battle of the Bulge, on our way back from Paris to the front, when we had a before Christmas dinner with them. Of course, it was very enjoyable to see them again.

After a few hours with the Uriet family, we then headed on to Reims, a beautiful city that is a champagne giant in France. We were again able to visit the Pommery winery and see the miles and miles of tunnels under the mountain where they store the champagne.

We had visited this winery when we came through Reims during the war, and they had generously given six of us GIs several bottles of their product. It is an impressive place, and the scenes in the tunnels seem to have been frozen in time.

After going to Paris, we went to London and out to Manchester and Moberly, where we had been stationed in England before going over for the invasion of France.

On yet another trip to Europe, Gene Abrams and I met Russ in Paris, and we went back to the beaches. Russ wanted Gene to photograph him wading ashore at the beach like General MacArthur did in the Philippines. I had a bad leg and could not walk that half-mile distance from the bluff where we parked down to the ocean and beach. So they took the camera equipment and went on down toward the beach.

I was standing there overlooking the sands and was leaning over a little bronze plaque that said, "Utah Beach." While I was watching Meyer and Abrams, a group of tourists came up. There was one man with a big "T" on his cap — possibly of the Uni-

Champagne Pommery Winery, 2000. Provided by Champagne Pommery, Reims, France. June, 2000.

versity of Tennessee or maybe Texas. He walked out in front of the group, turned to the lady next to him and said, "Now honey, there is where we came in — down there on Omaha Beach. My outfit landed right down there, and we came right up this hill here."

Well, I moved away from the little plaque that I had been standing by, and I said, "Sir, I am sorry, but you have the wrong beach. This is not Omaha; it's Utah Beach!"

Everyone in that crowd smiled really big, and some of them even giggled. He got back in the middle of this group and kept his mouth shut after that. The tour guide had a big grin on his face, too.

What I knew was that there was no way this man could have known where he came in on the beach. I had come in on this beach and had no idea of the spot where I had landed and neither did Russ or Gene.

Well, Gene got his picture of Russ wading ashore like MacArthur, and we went on our way again.

The Bridge

We had a frightening experience on this trip. We had rented a Mercedes and were making pictures along the way. Before the trip, I had had an accident in the foundry where I worked in Birmingham and had hurt my leg. I was on crutches most of the time to stay off of my feet as much as possible.

There are bridges over the autobahn in Germany to enable the farmers to cross this dangerous highway. We decided to park under one of these bridges and film some scenes from on top of it. We carried our big camera, the tripod and heavy belt with all the batteries in it up onto the bridge.

I did most of the shooting on this trip, and Abrams did most of the driving. He was supposed to drive down, turn around, come back and go on under the overpass. I was to film him driving the car under the bridge and then going on down the autobahn. He was then to turn around at the first exit and come back to pick us up. This was 4:00 in the afternoon.

Gene was not able to turn off at the first exit and thus had to go to the next one. When he took that exit, he went down and came back up on the autobahn going in the same direction from which he had come. He did not realize his mistake and kept looking for us standing on the little bridge. He looked at all these bridges on his route, but was unable to locate us any place. He had gone about 70 miles when it got dark, so he checked into a motel at Kassel. The motel was about $100.00 a night, but he never went to bed — he just walked the floor all night.

In the meantime, we were still back there on this bridge, and it started getting dark. We had all this heavy camera equipment with us, and we couldn't carry it down. Russ walked down to a place where he could call the police. When they came, they wanted to know what we were doing with all this camera equipment. We told them that we were taking pictures of this farmer out in the field cutting his corn into silage for feed. The police believed our story, so they loaded up all this camera equipment and took us to the only hotel in the little town of Hunsfeld.

We took a room, but we still did not know how to get in touch with Gene. We didn't know what had happened to him and were afraid he might have gotten lost and wound up in the Russian zone or wrecked. We called the hospitals in the area to no avail. Police over there are divided into districts, and Gene had driven out of one police district, through another and into a third. Of course, he did not know how to get in touch with us either.

Russ had left his briefcase in the car, and in the briefcase was a card with Hans Krause's name on it — the guy Russ had purchased the camera from on our earlier trip to Germany. However, the card only had an office number, not a home number. Russ, in the meantime, had called Hans at his home to tell him what had happened and that hopefully Gene would find the card and call. The next morning Gene did get in touch with Hans who told him to get back on the autobahn. We were to be waiting on the bridge for him.

While we had been waiting and worrying during all of this, Russ had begun to drink a great deal. Sometime during the night, he got sick and messed the bed. He didn't say anything about it but just covered it all up with the bed covers. The next morning, Gene came back and Russ was on the bridge waiting for him. When they got back to the hotel, we went down to check out and pay the bill. I saw Russ give the little maid a handful of German marks, and I wondered why he was tipping her that much. Then she looked at me as if to say, "You sorry so and so!"

As we were going down the road, Russ started laughing, and I said, "What's your trouble?"

He said, "Do you know why that little German maid looked at you with fire in her eyes? Well, I told her that it was you, not me, that had messed the bed."

We went back by Fort Driant, the fortress at Metz. We were going to make some pictures there, but the French Army had taken the place over and were using it as a training base. There was no way for us to get in there.

We stopped in Cheligny and began shooting scenes of the courthouse, the mayor's house and an office house. Some fellow on a bicycle stopped to talk with us, and he remembered when the American soldiers were there during WWII. He got in touch with the mayor, and the mayor got in touch with everybody.

House in Cheligny, France. Part of 166th Signal Photo Company lived here in January, 1945 — just after the Battle of the Bulge. This photograph taken by Sumners on a return visit to Europe, 1977. He and his friends were given a champagne brunch by the mayor during this visit to Cheligny.

They had a champagne brunch for Gene, Russ and me, which brought out the newspapermen and photographers who took our pictures for a story in their local paper. This really made us feel good to know that they did remember and cared about what we had done during the war.

The man on the bicycle gave us a fifth of Maribelle, which is somewhere in between Calvados and cognac. It would compare to peach brandy, but it's really stout.

Three or four nights later, we were staying in another location. We had gone to bed, and about three hours later something woke me up. There was a balcony that ran along the outside that connected to all the upstairs rooms. I got up and eased out on this balcony to see what had made the noise. Gene was out there.

He had drunk that whole fifth of Maribelle sitting out on the balcony and could not get up. I had quite a job getting this 6'7" drunk fellow back to his room and into bed. He had a huge hangover and was very sick the next morning. We still made him drive the car, even with his headache. We had a good time and shot a lot of scenes in the countryside.

Gene and I then flew back to the states after that, but Russ remained and Paul Fox, another soldier from our company, came over to help him shoot some more scenes.

My wife, Floyce, went with me on another trip to Europe, and we met Meyer in Munich, Germany. We rented a car and drove on into Berlin. On our trips before, we were not allowed to go into the Russian Zone because of the Berlin Wall and fences and other political things.

We had been able to photograph the fences before, and there was an area cleared off next to it that was said to be mined to keep East Germans from coming over to West Germany. There was a road that went down by there and it was patrolled every 30 minutes or so by an armored car. Guard posts were elevated some 50 feet up in the air with machine guns mounted on top. So we had not been able to get into the East Zone.

On this trip there was no evidence that a wall or fence had ever been there as they had cleaned the place up after removal of the Wall. This allowed us to go back into some of the towns where we had been during the war. In fact, we went back to Oberdorla, which is the town where I made my best combat picture.

This was a combat picture of tanks and combat troops going through the streets of Oberdorla. It was a coordinated air, tank, artillery and infantry attack, which inflicted a lot of casualties on the Germans. When Floyce, Russ and I were there on this trip, we found the same street where I had made the picture, and there were still bullet holes in the walls of the buildings.

This area's scenery had changed very little since World War II because this area in East Germany was under Communist rule, and they did not have the resources to make many improvements. Of course, after they combined the East and West, the money was available to repair some of these neglected areas.

They also had done very little work on the roads and bridges during all these many years, but were currently in the process of repairing some of them. We drove up to a place where the bridge was out so had to take a detour. Some 25 to 30 miles and an hour or so later, we came back up to the same road we had left, but on the other side of the river.

We then went on to Berlin, and it was a completely different world from the rest. It's a wide open city; they never seem to sleep as they have lots of activities going on all the time. We went to see many of the famous museums and buildings that we had heard of but had never visited.

The last time I went to Europe with Russ, I met him in Brussels, Belgium. I flew from Atlanta via Orlando to London where I was met by Stan Hark, Meyer's film distributor. We drove to the other airport and flew on to Brussels where Russ was being honored with showings of his films at one of the theaters there.

I had been on the planes and had had very little sleep in 30 hours. I was sitting there with several books in my lap while Russ was on stage handling the question and answer part of the program. I fell asleep and dropped the books, and it sounded like a bomb had exploded. Russ said, "Now that you are awake, Sumners, you come on up here. I want you to answer some of these questions." I got up and went up on stage to help him with the question being asked by the people in the audience.

When I was ready to fly back home, Russ didn't want me to leave and tried to get me to stay for another week. I told him I needed to get home, because I had been sick before arriving there. Russ had rented a car, and I told him I needed some kind of medicine to make me feel better. He said he knew just what I needed, so he stopped at a place and bought a fifth of cognac. I put it down in the floorboard of the car, and I sipped on

Charles Sumners and Russ Meyer (with camera) filming in Germany, Oct. 1979. The road turning left goes to German East Zone. Barricaded around the curve — no one could enter.

Russ Meyer, Floyce and Charlie Sumners at Sumners' home in Alabama, June 1986.

the cognac all day. The next day, Russ got me another fifth of cognac, and that kept me going, I guess.

Patton Memorial

This was not the best of the trips we had had together, but we had some meaningful experiences. We started back at the beaches and photographed all of General Patton's monuments and memorials all the way through Avranches to Luxembourg. The American Military Cemetery in Hamm, outside Luxembourg-City, is where General George S. Patton is buried with 5,076 soldiers of the Third Army. Major museums include Diekirch, Clervaux, Wiltz and Ettelbruck. The latter, dubbed "Patton Town" by its citizens, has a museum devoted to General George S. Patton in addition to a larger-than-life-sized statue of the general, a Patton tank and a towering obelisk.

We gave the man in charge of the cemetery a book, *Patton's G.I. Photographers*, edited by one of our buddies, Ralph Butterfield. We signed it and gave it to him for the museum. I'm sure people going through there will have the opportunity to browse through it; it's a good addition to the other items there.

At one time General Patton said that he wanted to be buried with his troops, and he was. But the enormous traffic to see his grave was making it difficult to keep the other GI graves in good order. So they moved his grave to the head of this cemetery, and he is now buried there with his marker. A rumor spread around that he had been moved to Arlington National Cemetery near Washington, D.C., but that is not true. His grave is still there in Luxembourg, along with those soldiers killed at the Battle of the Bulge.

It is a beautiful cemetery kept to perfection in every way, as were all of the cemeteries that we visited — from the beaches through France, Germany and into Luxembourg. Many years ago, the United States government established a cemetery fund to take care of all military cemeteries throughout the world. They are certainly doing an excellent job of maintaining them. All of them that we saw were beautiful, well-kept memorials to the men and women who paid the ultimate price and never made it home.

L–R: Russ Meyer, Jim Ryan, Billy Newhouse, Bill Cummings. Three World War photographs chosen for the International Combat Camera Association, Inc., collection. Top photograph and bottom photograph taken by Charles E. Sumners.

Normandy Beach Cemetery. October, 1979.

Epilogue

It has been said that the combat cameramen of World War II were the eyes of the battlefield, using their cameras to record the scenes for our country and the people back home. This was the most photographed war in history, and today these pictures stand as an important documentation of this period for posterity.

Kay Hively of the *Neosho Daily News* in Neosho, Missouri, observed: "The men of the 166th faced enemy fire as did other fighting men, but their job was to record the war and its events rather than return the firepower necessary to silence the opposing guns. They trudged all over Europe carrying both still and motion picture cameras right onto the front lines as well as the more quiet areas of occupation."*

Over half a century ago, I left home as a teenager and joined thousands of others from all over the world. We participated in an event that will forever mark a milestone in the history of mankind. Those of us who came home alive, returned different people from those who had left. We had traveled "roads" we never dreamed existed.

The experiences—although occurring in varied locations and being so different in many aspects for each of us—provided the one thing that we all shared in common ... *memories.*

*Neosho Daily News, November 6, 1985.

INDEX